GOING ABOVE AND BEYOND

Reach the Pinnacle of Customer Service
by Learning How to Think and Act
Like a Concierge

Other Books by Katharine C. Giovanni
The Concierge Manual
God, Is That You?

E-Books
The In-House Concierge Manual

Contributing Author
101 Great Ways to Improve Your Life: Volume 3

GOING ABOVE AND BEYOND

Reach the Pinnacle of Customer Service
by Learning How to Think and Act
Like a Concierge

By Katharine C. Giovanni

NewRoad Publishing   Wake Forest, NC

Published by

NewRoad Publishing
3650 Rogers Road, #328
Wake Forest, NC 27587

Tel: 919-453-2850
E-mail: info@NewRoadPublishing.com

First Edition
Copyright © 2009 by Katharine C. Giovanni

Library of Congress Control Number
2009930611

ISBN 978-1-931109-08-6

Printed in the United States of America

Cover Design/Layout by Candice Farrell

For Ron

The Nicest Man in the World

Acknowledgments

The following people have my deepest and most sincere thanks
for all the help they provided to me in writing this book.

First, thanks go to my family for giving me their love
and support! I couldn't do it without you guys.

To Candice Farrell: This book couldn't have been written without
you. The book cover you designed is outstanding, the interior lay-
out is perfect, and the advice you gave me was always spot on.

To Carla Mandell, who put up with me for months
as I was writing this book: Your assistance was invaluable,
and you have my eternal gratitude.

To Jackie Farley: I could never have written this
book without your patience and wisdom.

Special thanks to my extraordinary editor,
Sherry Roberts of The Roberts Group.

To Coco Giancana, Mike Wall, Stephanie Leese Emrich, Jill Preis,
Dallas Teague Snider, Leslie Graham, Erica Davis, and Doug Cook:
Your interviews are incredible and I can't thank you enough.

Katharine C. Giovanni, CCS

International Concierge Training Expert
Certified Concierge Specialist (CCS)
Author, Speaker, Consultant

Co-Founder of Triangle Concierge

Co-Founder and Chairman of the Board
International Concierge and Errand Association (ICEA)

The story begins decades ago, with a handful of pioneers — and Katharine Giovanni was one of them. If you looked around the United States back then, you might have found two dozen concierge services, but certainly no more than that. Sensing a need, Katharine propelled her meeting planning business into something more cutting edge: a company that could offer concierge services and products to an eclectic range of industries that had yet to discover the world of the concierge.

Katharine has gone from being a meeting planner and concierge for Fortune 500 executives to becoming one of the world's leading international concierge training experts. As Triangle Concierge's senior trainer and speaker, Katharine has taught workshops to groups, individuals, hospitals, small businesses, and large corporations. She is also the chairman of the board and cofounder of the International Concierge and Errand Association (ICEA), one of the first associations for the concierge industry.

A highly sought-after expert on the concierge industry, Katharine has both been interviewed by dozens of newspapers, magazines, radio, and television shows from around the country including The New York Times, The Washington Post, The Los Angeles Times, The Wall Street Journal, Time Magazine, Money Magazine, Forbes, Women's World Magazine, Condé Nast, Delta Airlines Sky Radio, WOR Radio, CBS News, ABC News, and ABC News Nightline.

A dynamic public speaker and a member of the National Speakers Association, Katharine has appeared at seminars and conferences around the county. She is an acclaimed author as well. Her titles include *The Concierge Manual, Going Above and Beyond*, and her inspirational book *God, Is That You?* In addition to publishing, Katharine is one of the designers of TriTrax, the world's premier concierge software.

Raised in New York City, Katharine earned a BA from Lake Forest College and currently lives in North Carolina with her husband Ron and two sons.

Katharine can be reached through her Web sites at www.triangleconcierge.com and www.katharinegiovanni.com.

Table of Contents

Introduction

I was searching the Internet for customer service articles a while back and do you know what I found? Dozens of them. I also found customer service consultants, customer service training seminars, and more books than I could count on the topic.

Here's my question: since the subject is so easily accessible and everyone is writing about it, then why are so many people complaining about the bad customer service they are receiving? Over the years, I've noticed that if I ask someone about customer services, they immediately tell me their "bad" customer service story. Everyone has one. Most have several.

I teach a lot of workshops around the country, and at one of them, I asked a group to give me some examples of bad customer service. Instantly, over a dozen hands shot up in the air. I called on several people, and we listened to their bad service examples.

I then asked the same group to give me a few examples of great customer service.

Silence. Not one hand went up. Not one! You could hear a pin drop. So I decided to tell one of my own to see if I could get the ball rolling.

I then asked the same question to the group again.

They just stared at me. The silence was deafening.

So I gave a few more great service examples and moved on.

The next month, I did the same thing with a completely different group in another city and guess what happened? The exact same thing! Unbelievable. Two groups who had NO stories about someone who gave them great customer service? Surely, this had to be a coincidence.

I tried again a few months later. This time one person raised her hand and told a story about the great service she received when she visited a particular restaurant. We'll ignore the fact that out of sixty people in the room, fifteen people raised their hands wanting to tell me their bad service stories. Incredibly, only one person in the entire group had a good customer service story.

What's going on? Is good customer service really dead?

Are we so into our technology that we've forgotten about the human element?

Are we so consumed with ourselves and what we are doing that we've forgotten how to treat each other?

What's happened to us? Have we forgotten what we were taught? Or were we just never taught it?

So where do you find incredible, over-the-top customer service?

Let me answer that by asking you a question: When you hear the word "concierge," what are the first thoughts that pop into your head?

- Extraordinary customer service?
- Someone who is able to get anything, at anytime, for anyone?
- A person who will immediately solve your problem and answer all your questions?

When you visit a hotel and walk up to the concierge, you can be absolutely positive that this person will be able to help you, no matter what your needs are. Nothing is too hard for him or her. You know with 100 percent certainty that customer service is the concierge's number one priority. This is the one person in the world who you expect will give you extraordinary customer service and will go above and beyond the call of duty.

Now, if you walk into a convenience store (no disrespect intended), do you expect extraordinary customer service?

You don't? Why not?

What if you do get that unbelievable service there? Are you shocked? Do you go back to the store again?

Of course, you do.

So why can't everyone be a concierge? You don't have to be a concierge to ACT like one! This is what this book is about. Concierge work is a lifestyle; it's a way of life. It's about how you treat people. It's about going that extra mile. You don't need to be a concierge; you just need to learn how to think and act like one.

Simply put, a concierge is not what we do; it's who we are. It's a twenty-four-hour-a-day, 365-day-a-year state of mind.

Let's start with the definition of a concierge. Exactly what is it? I think the short version here is that it is simply another word for personal assistant. A concierge will do anything for anyone, anywhere at any time as long as it's legal, moral and ethical.

It could also be said that the word "concierge" is another way of saying over-the-top customer service. In fact, most concierges around the world believe that customer service is something you should practice every minute of your life, not just once a year at the occasional customer service workshop.

The independent concierge industry itself was started several decades ago by a few brave pioneers who took the hotel concierge idea and decided to offer it to the mainstream world. I have been training concierges since 1998, and when I started, there were, perhaps, a few dozen concierge companies around the U.S. Today, I suspect there are thousands, and it's starting to sweep the world.

You can now find concierges everywhere— in hospitals, malls, corporations, apartment buildings, office buildings, airports, colleges, associations, churches, and on and on. Companies around the world are realizing that offering services that are geared toward gaining employee and customer loyalty is the key to their success. Exceeding customers' expectations has become the name of the game.

Now here's the real question: How do you offer unbelievable over-the-top customer service? How do you act? What do you do? What do you say?

The answer is that you learn how to behave like a concierge—and this book will teach you how to do just that.

Now I understand that many of the principles I'm talking about might seem basic to some of you. I also understand that there are many people who desperately need to hear these principles. In fact, I think that some of these principles are so incredibly important, I've mentioned them in more than one chapter. While you might think you don't need to read this book, a refresher course is always helpful as we all tend to forget what we learned long ago.

A few years ago, I held one of my two-day workshops designed to teach people how to start their own concierge business. As I was waiting to begin the class, a gentleman walked in and sat down. A few moments later, I went around the room and asked people why they were there. When we came to Joseph, he started to talk about his extremely successful concierge business in Washington, DC (1600 Concierge, Inc.). Stunned, I asked him why he was taking the class as it was immediately clear to me that he didn't need to be there. His answer was simple:

"Sometimes, in order to move forward, it's helpful to go back to the basics because with time comes complacency, and then we are back to mediocrity."

Exactly right.

Besides the basics, I have included some interviews I conducted with a few associates of mine who are all experts in their field. You'll be reading opinions from hotel concierges, independent concierges, lobby concierges, an international protocol expert, and my business partner Ron, who has been in the customer service field for more than thirty years. They all graciously shared their experience and wisdom with me, and their sage advice to all of you is something that you don't want to miss.

So where am I going to take you in this book?

Above and beyond anything you've ever known.

Are you ready?

Let's begin.

**If you are wrapped up in yourself,
you are overdressed.**

— *Kate Halverson*

Chapter One

The Great Secret of the Concierge Industry

My views on customer service are actually pretty simple. If you're rude to me, I'm certainly not going to want to use your product (or service) again. However, if you are nice to me and go out of your way to help, then I'm going to keep coming back and will recommend you to everyone I know.

I can't stress enough how important good customer service is to your business. It doesn't matter what business you are in, nor does it matter whether you are an employee, management, or the business owner, customer service should be your number one priority. Not only is it extremely professional, but people will go out of their way to come back and use your service if you are nice to them. In fact, studies have shown that people will drive out of their way, and even spend a little more money, if they know they're going to get superior customer service.

Clearly, the way you treat a client at first contact is critical because, like me, if they have a bad first experience, they'll never use your service or product again. Remember, there is no such thing as a second first impression. If you are rude to the customer and greet him or her with a bad attitude, will that customer want to come back? How do you think it will reflect on you and your business?

Here's the bottom line: treat everyone with respect, kindness, and honesty. These are basic customer service principles that everyone should apply to their business. You treat people the way that you would like to be treated—you show them the same dignity and respect you expect people to show you. To do that, you need to really listen to what they're saying. Ask open-ended questions and then be quiet so that you can hear their answers. Please do not talk over them! Try to do your best to refrain from interrupting someone when they're speaking.

Now please answer the following question for me. Who is the most important person in the company?

The CEO?

The president?

The answer is the person who the customer has contact with first.

The most important person in the company is the receptionist, the front desk staff, the doorman, valets, the person standing at the cash register in the front of the store—they are your most valuable assets. They are the front line and can make or break a sale in a heartbeat. With this idea in mind, I think it goes without saying that in order to provide superior customer service, you need to hire the right people. You need people who are already warm, friendly, and approachable; people who will smile and actually care about your customers.

This leads me to an industry secret that will change your life. It's an incredible secret that will propel you into a new and prosperous direction.

Ready?

Here's the greatest secret of the concierge industry:

JUST BE NICE.

I know it sounds simple, and you think I'm trying to be funny, but I'm actually serious. I'm also aware of the old adage, "Nice guys finish last." Funny thing is, it's not true. Nice guys finish first.

According to a study done at Harvard University in 2008, researcher David Rand found that nice guys really do finish first. Using the game "Prisoner's Dilemma," Rand gave one hundred Boston area college students the choice to punish their teammates whenever they behaved badly. Interestingly, the players who made the most money in the game were the ones who punished people the least. The ones who punished the most came in last.

A friend of mine did a similar experiment at a retreat he attended. Everyone was asked to form a circle. Each person was then given an equal amount of play money and told to give money to other group members. The person with the most money at the end of the game would be the winner. As the game progressed, some people were reluctant to give their money to others thinking that if they held back they would have the most money at the end. To everyone's surprise, the participant who gave the most money away the fastest ended up winning the game. What was even more astonishing is that this participant won even though he gave so much money away some of it was dropping on the floor.

So nice guys really do finish first after all.

There is a universal principle called the Law of Reciprocity that states, "What you put out, you'll get back." So if you put out integrity, love, and honesty, and you're nice to people, that's what you'll get back.

Now don't think I can't hear you naysayers out there doubting what you're reading. The bottom line is this: If you treat your customers badly, perhaps even yell at them, what do you think they're going to do back? How are they going to react? Will they come back and do business with you again? Will they talk nicely about you and your company to their friends?

If you are a business owner, how do your employees feel if you don't treat them well? If your employees are unhappy, how do you think these unhappy people will treat your customers? How does your staff treat each other? It should go without saying that the way employees are treated is exactly how they will treat their customers.

A truly great concierge treats everyone the same way—from customers to fellow staff members; a concierge is nice to everyone and treats them all with respect.

There is a lot of competition out there. Today's customers have no patience for horrible customer service and will simply take their business elsewhere. I actually have a client who started a concierge business because he received horrible service from a local concierge (like every industry, we have our share of companies that do not live up to high customer service standards). Now instead of being their client, he's their direct competition!

It's a competitive world, and everyone is trying to get to the top. So what do you think will put you there? The answer is customer service that goes above and beyond anything the customer has ever experienced.

Remember that old TV show Cheers? Everyone prefers to go somewhere where people know their name and greet them when they walk in the door. A welcoming atmosphere drives customer loyalty, boosts employee retention, and will increase the company's chance of long-term success. Conversely, an atmosphere where there is little customer service will actually lower client retention.

These facts lead me directly back to that industry secret I mentioned:

You have to be nice to people.

You need to be kind, warm, approachable, and understanding, and your tone has to be even and cheerful because if you're not, you'll lose the customer.

**About 70 percent of customers' buying decisions
are based on positive human interactions
with sales staff. The bottom line is that people
buy from people, not companies.**

— *Lee J. Colan, Passionate Performance*

Chapter 2

Kindness Leads to Loyalty

Key to Excellence:

Exceed their expectations.

Like many people, I regularly go to the chiropractor. In fact, I've been going to one for years.

Like many medical offices, my chiropractor has his share of staff turnover. Over the years, I've been greeted by all sorts of people, and most of them have been great. My doctor has a really good grasp of what great customer service should be, and it shows.

A while back, however, I arrived for my monthly appointment and was given a lukewarm greeting by the woman behind the desk. Since this sort of greeting is unusual for his office, I noticed it immediately. She said good morning to me (with no smile on her face whatsoever) and got me in to see the doctor in due course. Her motions were all mechanical, and she exhibited no warmth or interest in me at all. I actually felt like I was bothering her! As I sat and waited for the doctor, I noticed that no one in the office was smiling or joking around with each other like they usually did. In fact, there was a depressing and heavy feeling in the air. It was as if her attitude was infecting everyone who came in contact with her, and the energy in the office was horrible. It was contagious, and I'll admit that I wasn't in the best of moods when I left there.

Expecting the same receptionist the following month, I arrived at my chiropractor's office and took a deep breath as I opened the door. However, when I walked in, I was greeted by an entirely different person. This young lady was the complete opposite of the other receptionist. She was warm and friendly and smiled broadly at me the second I walked through the door. As I signed in, she amiably chatted with me and quickly ushered me into the office. As I sat and waited for the doctor, I noticed that every patient who left had a smile on his or her face. The receptionist was warm and friendly to everyone and seemed genuinely interested in each patient. A far cry from the previous month! I could actually feel the difference in the energy in the office. It was happier and felt lighter somehow. When I left, I had a smile on my face and felt happy.

Now which receptionist would you prefer to be greeted by? I know what my choice is.

Here's an even better question: How many clients would my doctor have lost had he kept that first receptionist? My guess is several.

One of the reasons why my chiropractor has a successful practice is because he and his staff are nice to people. People like going there because the chiropractor and his staff make them feel good inside and out, and the service is great.

Being nice to people creates customer loyalty.

I recently attended a seminar at the Disney Institute. Toward the middle of the day, the trainer began to talk about company loyalty and what makes customers loyal. As he strolled around the room asking people what makes customers loyal, the woman behind me quietly raised her hand. As she spoke, her story stunned the crowd into silence.

Her husband was laid off from his job, and they were trying to cut down their bills. So they started calling every company they could to lower their payments. Eventually, they decided to call their alarm company to turn the service off. When she got a customer service representative on the phone, she politely requested that the company cancel their service. The representative immediately asked, why, was the service bad?

No, she responded, and explained about her situation and the need to trim expenses.

The alarm company representative listened politely and then refused to turn off her service. Stunned, the woman asked why? The reply was incredible. The representative said not only did the company refuse to cut off her service, but it would keep her service on for free until her husband found a new job and they were back on their feet again.

Now that's customer service that goes above and beyond. What puts that company ahead of everyone else? It treats its customers like people— not like customers.

Here's another example, we were driving home to North Carolina, and it was late, extremely cold, and raining hard. Ron and I must have gotten off at a dozen exits looking for a hotel only to find them all full. Finally, we pulled into the parking lot of a Hampton Inn in Maryland. Crossing his fingers, Ron walked into the lobby and asked if there were any rooms available. A lovely young lady looked up and politely told him that the inn was full. She then asked him if he would like her to call the other hotels in the area to see if she could find him a room. She didn't have to do that, yet she did, and soon found us a room a few miles away in a competitor's hotel. I have to add here that none of the other dozen hotels we stopped at that evening offered to call around, she was the only one.

Her extraordinary kindness has led to our loyalty because now whenever we're on the road, we always stop at Hampton Inns whenever we can.

The Capital City Club

Ron and I have been training concierges for well over a decade now, and most of our training is conducted at the Capital City Club in downtown Raleigh, North Carolina. Now why do you suppose that Ron and I keep going back to the same club year after year?

Price?

The food (which is fantastic by the way)?

Location?

The answer is: Service.

It's a known fact that people will drive miles out of their way if they know that they're going to receive unbelievable customer service. Great service is clearly the key to a successful business, and no one does it better than the Capital City Club. Simply put, customer service that goes "above and beyond" is who they are, and it permeates every part of the club.

It starts the minute you step off the elevator and are greeted by the club's excellent concierge. From there, you'll walk down the hall and will find yourself being greeted with a smile and some warm words by every staff member you see. When you visit the ladies room, you might even meet the attendant Ophelia, whose infectious smile lights up the room.

The Capital City Club's secret? This incredible group of people treats everyone with kindness, respect, and dignity.

They also all call me by name. Never my first name, mind you, it's always "Mrs. Giovanni." (I'll speak more on this, and why it's so important, in chapter 4.)

I just love going to places where people treat me correctly, know my name, and make everything run smoothly. Whenever I'm there, it really feels like I'm a member of their family.

Their kindness has lead to my loyalty.

I remember one day in particular. I had to meet a client and was running a little late. Since I don't like to be late, I backed out of my driveway a little faster than I normally would. When I hit the brake to turn my car around, my entire cup of coffee spilled into my leather handbag. Since I was already late, I ran back into the house, threw the bag into the kitchen sink, grabbed another one (women always have more than one), and sprinted back to my car.

The day didn't get any better.

When I arrived at the Capital City Club, I met the client and sat down to begin the session. I then reached for the water pitcher and poured myself a glass of water, only to spill the entire glass on my client about twenty minutes later.

In all my years of working with clients, I've never done that. It really threw me. I apologized profusely.

While my client was in the ladies room attempting to dry off, I walked out into the hall and tried to compose myself. There, I ran into Linwood, one of the club's main dining room managers. He took one look at my face and immediately asked what was wrong. After telling him what had happened that day, he suddenly became my personal motivational coach. For five minutes, he encouraged me, motivated me, and completely turned my bad day around.

Feeling better, I walked back into the room and continued the training. About an hour later, the dessert chef knocked on the door. When I told him to come in, he politely greeted me and said that Linwood told him that I was having a bad day and to please accept this small token with his compliments. He then placed a platter filled with an incredible chocolate dessert on the table.

I just love chocolate, and, of course, all the folks at the Capital City Club knew that.

At 3:00 p.m., knowing how much I like tea, a staff member came in with a small pot of tea. Again, with the club's compliments.

Now that is customer service that goes above and beyond. It touched my heart and soul and filled me with warmth and gratitude.

Now here's the good part: Not only have I never seen any of the Capital City Club's staff have a bad day, but the club's staff really hasn't changed much in the decade that I've been teaching there.

Being an inquisitive person by nature, I decided to find out why. So I called Mike Wall, who is the club's private event director and is absolutely the best in the business. Not only did I want to know why the club's staff turnover was so low, but I was also curious how the club trained its staff. What did the managers say that caused absolutely every staff member to provide such unbelievable customer service? What was their secret?

Here is his answer in his own words.

People Appreciate Good Customer Service

An Interview with Mike Wall, Private Event Director
The Capital City Club, Raleigh, North Carolina

Mr. Wall has been in the hospitality industry for more than eighteen years. His concentration at the beginning of his ClubCorp career was in service management, but he has been employed as the private event sales director of the Capital City Club in Raleigh since early 2001.

You have a staff that has been here for as long as I've been coming here. What is your secret to your employees' loyalty?

I think it's internal more than external. We are very close, mostly because we've been together for such a long time.

So you treat them like family?

Exactly. It's a family, and that's the way it's structured. If someone has a problem, they can come to us and we'll help them out. I think that's one of the key components as to why this company is so successful. It's not like other places because it's comfortable internally. We take care of each other. I remember when someone's house burned down. We all pitched in and helped them get back on their feet. Treating employees like family is the key.

How do you train the staff because I have to tell you that they're phenomenal! I've had people come for consultations from all over the world, and they have all told me that they've never experienced customer service like they get at your club.

I think the other key component that is drilled into everyone who works here is this—we teach everyone that every member and guest is to be treated like a king or queen. It's really the old adage that the customer is always right.

You never know what the member's or guest's perspective is, so you try to look at the situation from their point of view. We never ever just say "no, I'm sorry." We constantly remind our employees about customer service and remind them to treat the members like royalty absolutely every day. If it's something that the employee can't help with, then he or she knows to immediately find someone who can help the member. No one here ever says "no."

You teach your employees the right way, and you treat them the right way. So those two things combined is the secret behind your club's success?

Absolutely.

There's one focus that I think a lot of people lose, especially in their business. They forget to take care of the people who are actually buying from them. Take care of your customers, especially the repeat customers, because they're even more important. That's the only way that you can be successful. If you do things for people, and you take care of them well, then they're going to come back. If you don't, then you're going to lose them. That's what sustains us.

You also don't get thanked often do you? Years ago when I first started training clients at your club, I would go and seek out the people who worked the meeting for me to thank them (and I still do). They would always look at me strangely. When I questioned them, they told me that they rarely get thanked. I think that's sad.

Yes, that's true. Unfortunately, most of the time, it's a thankless job. You rarely ever hear if things went well; you only hear when they don't. It doesn't matter though; we still give 150 percent customer service.

That's exactly why you are so successful.

We're a family that treats our members and guests like royalty. That's the key. You need to concentrate on what you're providing and what makes you a success. We try to keep our focus on that. We focus on great service—great service for our employees and great service for our members and guests.

I don't think people realize how important it is to be nice. Even if you're not in a good mood, the real key is to still be nice to people. You don't do things just for the money.

I know that you plan a lot of weddings and both private and corporate functions. What do you do if someone gets angry?

Smile and kill them with kindness. We remind the staff that if members/guests get upset, it's not because they don't like you; it's most likely because they're under a lot of stress. They have a big weight on their shoulders, and once it's lifted they'll be as nice as they can be. You move forward, get things done as fast as possible, smile, and kill them with kindness.

Any last pieces of advice?

Remember, people appreciate good customer service. Everywhere you go, you need good service. You can't do things on your own. You can't go anywhere out there, buy anything, rent anything, or purchase anything without people helping you.

There are no traffic jams along the extra mile.

— Roger Staubach

Chapter 3

Your First Impression Should Be the BEST

Key to Excellence:

You need to go five steps beyond, not just one.

Have you ever heard of a second impression?

No? Well, here's another question for you: Did you know that you only have about ten seconds to make a great first impression?

Seriously, I'm not kidding. People will size you up in seconds! From the way you are dressed to the way you talk, people only need about ten seconds to get an impression of you. So you better make it a good one because you won't get a second chance.

If you want to be a truly great concierge, then you need to be aware of how you speak, how you dress, and what your body language is saying to people so that someone's first impression of you is fantastic.

Don't Judge a Book by its Cover

Before I talk about speech, manners, etiquette, and image, I would like to remind you about something that many of you were taught as a child:

Don't judge a book by its cover.

Although I just told you that your first impression is crucial, it's also important that you not judge people, even though they are obviously judging you. I'm completely aware that I just contradicted myself, but hear me out.

When I was a little girl, my mother gave me some wise advice that I carry with me to this day. It has served me well over the years, and it's a code that I live by:

*Just because other people are behaving badly and judging you,
it doesn't mean that you have to do the same. Be above it.
Rise higher. Two wrongs do not make a right.*

A truly great concierge learns to treat everyone with respect and kindness, no matter what. Always put your best foot forward. From how you personally dress and act, to how you talk to people, you should always treat everyone with dignity, respect, and kindness.

Years ago, when Ron and I were building our first home, I decided to do a little house hunting to see if there was anything else out there for us. I just wanted to make sure we were doing the right thing before we signed on the dotted line.

So one sunny day, after driving around for a while, I found myself in an attractive neighborhood only a few miles from the house we were building.

I soon found the Realtors that were selling homes in the area, parked my car, and walked in. The receptionist greeted me nicely and asked me to please sign in, which I did. She then handed me a packet of information. As I sat down, I noticed that it was an extremely well-appointed office with expensive furniture and artwork.

So I sat there and waited for the receptionist to send an agent over to chat with me about their neighborhood.

I sat for over thirty minutes.

Everyone ignored me, and those who were not with customers talked among themselves while I grew roots under my chair.

Fed up, I left and went home.

When an agent called the following week, Ron answered the phone. After listening to the agent for a minute or two, he reported how rudely I had been treated me and told the agent we weren't interested in the neighborhood. The agent had the class to apologize, but it didn't change the fact that we had moved on and weren't interested any longer.

Why did they ignore me?

It was how I was dressed. I wore a simple white t-shirt, faded old blue jeans, and some old white sneakers. I suppose they didn't think

I could afford a house. Unfortunately, their lack of good judgment caused them to lose a sale.

Never assume.

Years ago, a friend of mine owned a jewelry store in Pennsylvania. One day in late December, she watched an unkempt man walking down the street. His clothes were torn and ripped, and his face and hands were dirty. As she stood in the doorway of her shop, she watched the man enter and exit one store after another, always only staying a few minutes.

When he finally arrived at my friend's jewelry store, she welcomed him into the store with some warm words and a huge smile. She then walked over to the counter and asked how she could help. After quietly looking at the display case for a few seconds, he asked if he could see some jewelry and then proceeded to pull a wad of cash out of his pocket.

You see, he was a coal miner who had just been paid, and all he wanted to do was buy a present for his wife.

His dirty and disheveled appearance caused everyone else to ignore him when he walked into their shops. The good news is that he referred all his friends to my friend's store because she was so nice to him and gave him such incredible customer service.

The moral? Never judge a book by its cover. Don't make assumptions based on people's appearances because they just might surprise you. I want you to do this in spite of the fact that they are judging you.

How would you talk to the CEO of a Fortune 500 company?

What would you say to Oprah if she walked into the room right now?

How would you act?

How would you speak to the maître d' of a five-star restaurant?

That's exactly how you should speak to everyone, no matter who they are, what they do, or even what they look like.

Here's another important thought:

Never assume the person who answers the phone is the lowest person on the totem pole. You might be speaking to the CEO.

If you call my office at Triangle Concierge, eight out of ten times you'll get me as I answer my own telephone. Somewhere around 2002, I was working at my desk when the phone rang. Normally I'll answer the phone by saying, "Good morning, Triangle Concierge, this is Katharine; how may I help you?"

However, on that particular afternoon I was busy writing and was distracted, so I just answered the phone with a short, "Triangle Concierge, may I help you?"

On the other end of the phone line, I suddenly hear a man say the following. I swear this is true; you just can't make this stuff up.

"Hello, honey. Could you be a doll and connect me to your boss? I have some important information for him, so if you could be a good girl and be quick about it, I'd really appreciate it. There's a good girl."

You can imagine what went through my mind as I listened to this guy, and it's not polite. In fact, I'll wager a guess that every woman reading this is having the same thoughts that I did on that afternoon.

When he finished his chauvinist speech, I could have let him have it, but I have to tell you that I was so angry that I really couldn't speak. So I just said two words, "Please hold," and I pressed the hold button. Okay, I'll tell you the truth, I actually pounded the hold button and threw the phone into its cradle.

I then walked down the hall to Ron's office. I'm not sure that my feet touched the ground I was so irritated. When I got there, I yelled at poor Ron and told him what happened. He calmed me down and told me that he'd take the call, which he did moments later. He let the guy go on for a while and listened to his sales pitch. After a few minutes, he politely interrupted him and said, "You know, you have quite a nice product, and our president might be interested in it, but, unfortunately, she was the one who you treated so badly on the phone just now. So I'm positive that she won't take your call."

We never heard from him again.

A few years later, Ron caught a similar call. One afternoon, the phone rang. Ron answered it only to be greeted by silence and a clicking sound. Since no one said anything back, he hung up as he was busy working. The phone rang again, and again he hung up when he was greeted with silence. The phone rings a third time, and this time Ron got distracted and the call went through. After he politely said, "Triangle Concierge, this is Ron, may I help you?" he heard a young man scream into the phone:

"HOW DARE YOU HANG UP ON ME? THAT WAS SO RUDE. I CAN'T BELIEVE YOU DID THAT."

He actually went on for a few minutes. Ron calmed him down by explaining that since he heard silence, he just assumed that someone misdialed. He apologized profusely several times, and then told the caller he was transferring the call to me.

When Ron arrived in my office, he was furious. In his thirty years of customer service, he had never gotten yelled at like that. So I took the call and politely listened to the guy. It turns out that he was a salesman who wanted to sell us a product. I let him go on for about a minute, and then said the following:

"You know, it sounds like you have a great product, but the gentleman who makes the decisions about that was the person whom you just yelled at. I'm positive that he won't talk to you now, but I wish you success."

Silence. Then a moment later I heard a gasp.

"Oh no, that was Ron? Oh my gosh. I'm so sorry. What can I do to make up for it? I'm having a bad day and didn't mean it. I'm so sorry! Oh my gosh."

You just can't make this stuff up.

Since I knew Ron was burning mad and would most likely not want to have anything to do with the salesman, I said, "I'm sorry, but you've burned the bridge on this one, but I do wish you good luck."

The moral of these stories? Never assume you know who is answering the phone. No one, no matter who they are, deserves to be treated badly. A truly great concierge intuitively knows this and will treat everyone with respect, kindness, and love—100 percent of the time—no exceptions.

Know Your Client's Expectations

An Interview with Coco Giancana
The Professional's Concierge, Las Vegas, Nevada

Ms. Giancana has been in the concierge business for the past twenty-five years, both as a business owner and a four-star hotel concierge. She is the founder and president of The Professional's Concierge in Las Vegas, Nevada.

When you are training your staff, what is the number one thing you tell them to do?

I've always had a motto, and it's something that I tell everyone I train. You should approach each and every moment as an opportunity to provide unparalleled service. Be determined to leave a lasting impression and gain a client for life. I always stress that a concierge should both build new skills and hone the old skills that you already possess.

To be a concierge, you need to conduct yourself with confidence, grace, efficiency, know-how, poise, style, and an exceptional level of attention to detail. A concierge knows what move should come next in any work-related situation. Successful concierges are confident enough to overcome any etiquette indecisions. They function with confidence and finesse, and they are always making a positive impression.

Another important point is to discover exactly what your client expects. You must know all the "when's" and "how's" so you can positively impact the expectations of your client. One of the most important things is to understand your client's expectations. Give your client your best. The treatment of the client must be custom tailored. Plus, in order to understand clients' expectations, concierges have to know ALL the facts. They have to make the client feel extremely important, respected, attended to, and comfortable. Most important, concierges have to offer their clients their undivided attention with a positive attitude. They must show genuine concern for the people they're dealing with, be discreet, and fulfill requests in a timely and professional manner.

Concierges should create a climate of acceptance. That comes through listening, identifying the client's wishes, being honest, and following through with every promise you make. A "great" concierge always delivers superior and exceptional service. Plus, a concierge always makes sure that clients fully understand what you can do for them. To be a really "great" concierge, you must be an extraordinary listener and ask targeted and specific questions. Concierges are prepared for every single encounter.

What kind of preliminary work can concierges do? How do they prepare?

Generally, if you are employed in a hotel, you will know who your assigned clients are going to be the next day. You meet with the head concierge to determine the best strategy in handling the clients and their every need. If it's a privately owned company like mine, you will come to me and ask questions and receive the necessary information you'll need to create an outstanding experience for the client. As the owner, I'm going to tell you things such as:

- Who the client is
- What company the client is affiliated with
- The client's position within the company
- The manner in which you should speak to the client
- The client's preferences, absolute needs, dislikes, or any quirks
- The level of individual care expected
- The type of personality (i.e., rude, sweet, easy to get along with, demanding, etc.)

These are some of the things that I want my concierges to prepare for. Concierges need to know who they're dealing with the next day so they can provide exceptional attention to all the details.

Consider Oprah's talk show. She invites a guest author to come on the show, and they discuss the book. Oprah reads the book the night before, then she reads something about the author. When she sits down with the author, she makes the author feel comfortable and treats the author like he or she is the only person in the room. Oprah knows which questions to ask, and how to behave when she's with a guest. I want my concierges to be polished professionals. They have to develop a long-term profitable relationship. They know to keep their clients' sensitive personal information private. People will become close to you, and you'll be privy to a lot of things concerning your client. It's imperative your business is the height of discretion!

How do you handle more than one person at a time?

You must learn how to juggle more than one client because you undoubtedly will find yourself doing more than one thing at a time. Most concierges have written "personal" e-mail responses on their computer, so they can send responses fast, such as "I am currently with another client, and I'll be with you in a minute." They will be the first person you answer, make them feel special. Most people will not expect you to hang up on the person you're speaking with on the phone (unless, of course, the client is angry, upset, or freaking out about something that just happened). If this happens, you must politely ask the person on the phone if you may place him or her on hold for a minute as you have a minor emergency. Don't let the client stay on hold for longer than a minute. You'll have to use your skills to gain information from the second client quickly. Find out what the emergency is, promise to fix it fast, and get the caller's phone number. Then return to the guest you placed on hold. Remember, know the client expectations, know all the facts about everybody you are dealing with and follow through. Never promise something you can't do. The client doesn't care about your excuses or why something hasn't been done; the client just wants it done. A concierge must provide quick solutions to his or her clients' unique challenges.

How much of your own personality can you infuse into a conversation with a guest?

You have to establish a superb rapport with your clients. You have to determine their needs and preferences by listening and responding to the cues they give you concerning how personal they want you to become. Some concierges will become extremely personal with their clients, telling them about their private life. I'm from the old school. I don't believe in that. I would rather have clients talk about themselves. I keep my conversation professional. I study their personality, their body language, listen to their requirements, and I give them my undivided attention. I want clients to feel special and know that I value their time. I'm constantly letting them talk. I'm responsible for entertaining the client and satisfying his or her every whim. You have to treat your client like royalty.

People today are smarter. They have access to all these resources on the Internet. Concierges need to understand the importance of their role in the cultivation and care of the client. Clients can shop anywhere in the world, so why should they choose you? Why do they need a concierge? Whether you're a hotel concierge, an independent concierge, or you work in retail, you're selling a relationship of personal care, attention, and loyalty so your clients will have the best experience possible. The way you provide your services to your clients is critical to reinforcing the integrity of the concierge. You have to arm yourself in both dress and demeanor in a way that will positively reflect your company's image. You have to be articulate, and you have to learn how much of your personal style you can integrate into your conversations with the guest. I also believe you should maintain an appropriate level of courtesy and formality.

I did some research when I was starting my business. I read that nationally, one out of four clients give low ratings for a service they've been provided, and of those clients who were disappointed with the service, only 5 percent will actually say something. The other 95 percent prefer to just switch companies. Clearly, good service is critical. Personally, I'll drive twice as far for something if I know I'm going to be treated like royalty and get great service. Clients don't want to hear you complain, nor do they want to know personal things about you unless they ask you a direct question. You're building a business relationship. You need to downplay your responses and keep it short. You don't see waiters getting too personal with guests. Most of them don't say things such as: my car broke down, I can't pay my rent, I had to take my sick dog to the vet. Clients don't want to hear that! Let the guest do the talking. Be quiet, listen, and empathize. My three favorite words as a concierge are: discreet, exclusive, and confidential. It really boils down to treating clients how they wish to be treated. It's all about them, not you.

What is the most important skill that a concierge needs to have?

To build a solid and trusting relationship with a client, you need to explore the client's expectations. Then go five steps beyond it. You need to know how to tailor your service approach to meet the client's individual needs. This will improve the likelihood the client will be loyal to you and stay with you for life. Your client needs to think, "No one else is going to be able to treat me like this. I couldn't possibly think of going somewhere else." Even if you don't work for a high-end store or a five-diamond hotel property, you can still behave like a professional concierge.

A concierge also needs to know how to greet people, when to pass along business cards, what to do if the person's name escapes you, proper business attire, how to host international clients, and how to write proper correspondence including e-mails, notes, and messages. You must learn what to do (and not do) on the telephone, and how to behave in social situations. These are only a few skills you need to have.

I have this written on my business cards: "Offer uncompromising service with uncommon discretion." To be a great concierge, you have to take those extra steps to find out what else you can do for your clients besides the basics. Remember, as a great concierge, you will have the power and the contacts to turn their dreams into their reality.

If you would like to reach Ms. Giancana, please e-mail her at
TheProfessionalsConcierge@cox.net

Chapter 4

Speech: What to Say and How to Say it

Key to Excellence:

Become an expert at speaking to people.

All great concierges speak and write well. If you do not speak properly, no matter which language you speak, you will not be taken seriously.

If the thought of speaking in public sends shivers down your spine as you read these words, then I suggest that you visit www.toastmasters.org. This great organization will teach you how to speak in public. Just visit the Toastmaster Web site to find a group near you. Also, many community colleges and universities offer noncredit courses in public speaking. Or explore your local bookstore, where you'll find some wonderful books written on the subject.

Why am I suggesting that you do this? Because in order to ACT like a concierge, you need to know how to speak to people. It goes beyond manners and saying "please" and "thank you." You need to speak in a language that everyone understands, while being warm, friendly, and approachable. People need to understand you.

A while back, I took my two teenage sons to a fast food restaurant. It was a rare outing as we generally don't eat fast food; however, we had been shopping and they were hungry. I pulled up to the drive through and a voice came over the speaker: "Your order," the restaurant employee snapped angrily into the speaker. No please, no pleasant voice, no nothing.

"I'd like a number two combo, please," I said politely.

"That's it?" she shouted. Her voice was a high-pitched whine, and she barked it at me like a drill sergeant. The tone reminded me of the cackle the wicked witch made in the Wizard of Oz.

"No, I'd also like a number three please," I said.

"That's it?" she shouted rudely again.

"No, I'd like two shakes, please," I said through gritted teeth. I was getting annoyed now.

"That's it?" she yelled again in the same horrible tone.

"That's it," I snapped. I had to really fight back the urge to yell it at her.

When I pulled up to the window, she silently thrust out her hand for the money. Once I gave it to her, she practically threw the bag out the window and offered no thank you.

Since I just couldn't let it go, I said, "You know, it's customary to say thank you to the customer," and drove away. My two sons just sat in the backseat laughing hysterically in disbelief. They were as stunned by her rude behavior as I was. I think the worst part was when one of my son's noticed that her uniform was different from everyone else's, meaning, of course, that she was the manager. I was speechless when he pointed this out to me.

Now, what she should have said instead of barking "that's it"?

How about: "Would you like anything else today?" or "May I get you anything else?"

Do you think I'll go back to that restaurant any time soon?

Would you?

As I said, you need to learn how to speak to people. I think the real tragedy here is that that employee probably thought she was being polite. I think that is how most people feel. They really do think they're being polite.

One of the most common mistakes I see is the "monotone" voice. These people will talk to you in a steady and even voice with no emotion in it. It's like they're robots with no feeling.

My recent visit to a doctor's office is a great example of this. When I walked in, the receptionist greeted me flatly, barely made eye contact, and told me to sit down until my name was called. She was cold, her motions were stiff, and she delivered her words to me in a monotone voice. You could tell that she really didn't want to be there. When I got to the exam room, the nurse spoke to me in a sterile tone, never looked up from her notes, didn't smile, and was neither warm nor friendly. I felt like a piece of machinery on a conveyer belt in a factory. I walked out shaking my head.

How do you think I felt when I left there? Do you think I went back?

The doctor could be the best in the world, but if his staff is rude to you and doesn't seem to care about you, then patient retention will suffer.

Here are a few tips:

Stand directly in front of the person you are speaking to with your shoulders squarely facing theirs.

When you are speaking with someone, your body should squarely face the person in front of you. You then look the person directly in the eye, introduce yourself in a clear voice, and offer a firm handshake. Also make sure that you respect the other person's comfort zone and stand about two to three feet away from him or her.

Don't interrupt them!

Please remember to start speaking AFTER the other person has stopped talking. In fact, wait a beat or two just to make sure that the other person is really finished and then talk.

Don't touch them.

Simply put, the only respectful place to touch someone is the hand when you are shaking it. Don't slap a person on the back or touch his or her arm.

Do not use bad language of any kind—no cursing!

I think it goes without saying that you shouldn't use foul language. Keep your voice calm at all times and never, ever, lose your temper. No exceptions. I don't care what the other person is saying. Stay calm and keep your voice level. Don't raise it under any circumstances. In fact, I've found that keeping my voice calm often gets my point across faster than if I was yelling at the person.

<u>Never</u> address them by their first name.

How many times have you pulled up to the drive-up bank teller, and she immediately called you by your first name? Or, after you've handed your credit card to the cashier, he says, "Thank you, Susan."

When I walked into a client's office a while ago, the receptionist (whom I had never met before) asked me to sign in. She then looked at my name and greeted me by saying, "Katharine, please have a seat. We'll be right with you." As I turned away to find a chair, there was a gentleman standing right behind me. He walked up to the window and signed in. The receptionist then looked down at his name and greeted him by saying, "Mr. Smith, please have a seat."

Excuse me? Why is she on a first name basis with me and not him? I'm sure that there was a logical explanation for this lapse in judgment, so I'll let it go. I think you get my point.

Here's another example. Every time I go through the bank drive-through near my home I get addressed differently. Sometimes I'm greeted with a "Good morning, Katharine" and other days it's "Hello, Kathy." My personal favorite came just the other day when I was making a deposit for my company, Triangle Concierge. When I drove up and sent the deposit through, the teller greeted me with a "Hello, Triangle." I was stunned, and not in a good way.

I think what irritates me the most is that whenever my husband goes through the drive-through, he's greeted as "Mr. Giovanni" every time. I find it simply incredible that, after all these years, men and women are still treated differently.

I just can't stress this enough, a truly great concierge who is offering first class service will NEVER call you by your first name.

Unless they give you permission, always address clients as "Mr. Smith" or "Mrs. Smith." If you don't know their last name, then please address the men as "sir" and the women as "ma'am." If they are from the United Kingdom or anywhere outside of the United States, then it's even more critical as Europeans are much more formal than we are in the U.S. So the rule is to never use someone's first name, until they give you permission and say to you, "Please call me Katharine."

One last thing here, please refrain from shortening clients' names. Don't assume that just because a client's name is Elizabeth, she'll like to be called Liz. It's rude to assume. Please ask first.

Please don't say "you're welcome" ever again.

I'll bet you didn't expect to see that in this book. Here's what I want you to say instead:

"It was my pleasure."

Now why do I want you to do that?

Mostly because no one else does. When is the last time you heard someone respond with an "it was my pleasure"? Most likely, you were at a five-star hotel or an expensive restaurant. These establishments completely understand that these small words will set them apart from all the rest. It gives them an edge. It's a gracious response that is above and beyond normal words.

"It was absolutely my pleasure."

Simple words that will propel you above and beyond average service.

Recently, I went to a takeout restaurant with my teenage sons, who always seem to be eating. When we placed our order, the server just gave us the food and then moved on to the next person. No thank you, no smile, nothing. Although I said thank you when she gave me the food, she just looked at me and said, "Next!"

We won't even talk about employees who say thank you to you as they look down at the cash register. Eye contact, people!

Actually, one of the few fast food restaurants that I will go to is Chick-fil-A, a company that has a well-known reputation for great customer service. Whenever I go there, I am always welcomed when I walk up to the counter and thanked when I leave. Recently, a girl even said, "It was my pleasure" to me. I was in heaven.

Concierge Work Is a Lifestyle

An Interview with
Stephanie Leese Emrich, Chef Concierge
The Talbott Hotel, Chicago, Illinois

Stephanie Leese Emrich celebrates her twenty-fifth year in hospitality, with five years as a hotel concierge. She is designated les clefs d'or and is the past president of the Chicago chapter of the National Concierge Association. Stephanie is a third-generation hotelier and hospitality educator, and has authored and instructed event planning courses for Lexington College in Chicago.

How do you teach concierges to act? What do you say to them?

Energy and consistency are important. The first thing I tell people is that this is not a glamorous job. You're standing all the time. In fact, most four- and five-diamond hotel concierges are on their feet on a marble floor. We are there to be at attention. You wouldn't pass a museum security guard sitting in a chair. Are they less effective while seated? Perhaps. It depends on the person. I do my best work when I'm face-to-face with our guests. We need to rise to the occasion, as in our posture, and be at eye level.

When advising newcomers, I suggest they figuratively place themselves on the other side of the desk. To best serve our guests, it is imperative to try to understand what is important to them. What I tell my trainees is to never address guests by their first name, even if they mention it. It is entirely too casual. Other guests might get a wrong impression and think that the person I'm speaking with works in the hotel. We have a guest who insists that we call her by her first name, and I will greet her instead with "How is our avid theater-goer this morning?" I have omitted using her first name to maintain consistency.

Concierges need to pretend they are walking into an environment like Disney World. When you get a call to be a Disney "cast member," you must assume a specific persona. There is a certain expectation from visitors as to how the place looks and feels. We are part of that look and feel. We become their experience.

Working in the hospitality field means you can't bring the other aspects of your life into that moment. You should leave behind your personal judgments. Focus on the guests and what they really want and need from you. Even though they seek our advice, inserting our personal preferences is not as valuable as answering the question from their perspective.

To make everyone's experience consistent, it's best to establish systems to operate efficiently. This starts with greeting every guest with the same sincere message. Consistency provides a reliable format. You then do not have to take the time and energy to question if you did the right thing. If you constantly work at the core elements of your service standards, it goes much further than trying to invent a new way each time. After the initial greeting, then you can modify your dialogue. If you are serving a repeat guest, you can alter it a bit with:

"You've been with us a number of times."

"We always appreciate your loyalty to our hotel."

"We know this isn't your first visit here. How can we make this one the best yet?"

You may wish to have a follow-up question, an up-sell so to speak. At a recent restaurant opening, we were given a marvelous seafood entrée, but none of the servers mentioned a potato or vegetable as a side. I immediately thought, "They just lost money." Since all the sides were extra, I kept thinking it was odd that they would not attempt to increase revenue, and at the very least complete the dining experience. Using that same mentality, I often think, what am I leaving on the table? What am I not doing? When a gentleman calls and asks for champagne for his date, I cannot imagine not suggesting that he accompany this beautiful bottle with chocolate-covered strawberries, flowers, and whatever else is appropriate. I thrive on asking the next question: What else may I help you with? How else may I assist you?

So you take everything one step further? For example, you not only give them a suggestion of where to have dinner, but you also offer to make them a reservation, show them where it is on a map, call them a taxi.

Absolutely. It's the complete experience that our guests should walk away with. You have to be at your best, but you also need to be who you are. That is one of the benefits of being in hospitality. Whether it's in retail or in a hotel, whatever the backdrop is, people want to see a personality beyond the uniform. You don't want to over-do it, so it is a very fine line. Just show them enough to make a connection and then let it be about them. It is great fun when you converse about their city or their profession, and they say, "Oh, so you know something about this?" They almost seemed surprised that you understand geography or are fluent on an array of topics. They are impressed with the way you have reached into their world.

If someone comes up to the desk and you're on the phone, what do you do?

This one is difficult. I try to always nod and raise an index finger to signal "one moment please," or raise an eyebrow to make eye contact so they know I've recognized that they have a need. Even though you and I both know that in between their request and the request waiting on the phone, you've just received a fax or an e-mail about something that is probably more time sensitive than all of it put together. It's all about making that person feel that they've been heard. If you go to a bank and you are in what seems an excessively long line, it's heart-warming when the banker looks over the top ledge and says, "We're going to be with everybody in a moment." Now everything is okay. They've seen you. The worst thing would be when you finally get to the front of the line, and the banker puts up the "closed" sign.

When guests approach your desk and you are on two phones at once, at the very least you must acknowledge them. In my case, because they are staying in the hotel, I might say, "May we phone you in your suite within the next fifteen minutes?" Offer them a specific return time and stick to it. Don't overpromise and underdeliver. Even with the best of intentions, some other task will distract you. Aim to underpromise and overdeliver. If I state fifteen minutes and I call them in ten, their expectations have been exceeded. This is the ultimate goal of a concierge.

What piece of advice do you have for new concierges?

Concierge work is a lifestyle. It can be long hours that can take all of you, but with countless rewards, heartfelt stories about bringing people together, and lifelong friendships.

A customer is the most important visitor on
our premises, he is not dependent on us. We are
dependent on him. He is not an interruption
in our work. He is the purpose of it. He is not an
outsider in our business. He is part of it.
We are not doing him a favor by serving him.
He is doing us a favor by giving us an
opportunity to do so.

— *Mahatama Gandhi*

Chapter Five

The Handshake

Key to Excellence:

Always mind your manners; there are no exceptions.

The Handshake

According to a study conducted by the University of Alabama, "There is a substantial relation between the features that characterize a firm handshake (strength, vigor, duration, eye contact, and completeness of grip) and a favorable first impression." The results of the study show that "those with a firm handshake were more extraverted and open to experience and less neurotic and shy than those with a less firm or limp handshake."

In short, a great first impression can be squashed in a heartbeat by a bad handshake.

One way a handshake was defined can be found on www.Wikipedia.org:

> A handshake is a short ritual in which two people grasp each other's right or left hands, often accompanied by a brief up and down movement of the grasped hands. Its origins are unclear, although Philip A. Busterson's seminal 1978 work "Social Rituals of the British" traces its roots back to Sir Walter Raleigh, claiming he introduced the custom into the British Court during the late sixteenth century.

The most popular theory on when people started shaking hands with each other seems to be that it started way back in medieval Europe, where shaking someone's right hand would prove that you were not carrying a weapon. Since most people were right-handed, this gesture told people that you weren't going to kill them. It was a symbol of trust.

In today's world, the handshake is now considered to be a symbolic gesture of peace. One of the most famous handshakes was the "handshake that made history." On April 25, 1945, United States and Soviet Union forces met on a bridge in Germany and shook hands with each other. They linked up to fight Germany. Another historical handshake that many people call "the turning point of twentieth-century history" occurred when President Richard M. Nixon and

Chairman Mao Zedong of China shook hands with each other, thus ending the breach between the United States and China. History is filled with hundreds of stories about people from different backgrounds coming together and shaking hands in one life-changing moment.

Why?

Because in that brief moment of time—they are equal.

Recently, I met a speaker named Donna Cardillo, who wrote a great article about handshakes entitled "The Uncommon Handshake." In her article she states that:

> *While men have traditionally been socialized to shake hands with other men, women, for the most part, have not. Handshaking customs have changed over the years. Many men of an older generation were taught to use one type of handshake with a man and another, more delicate version with a woman. Likewise, in the past, men did not extend their hand to a woman unless she extended her hand first. Some women of an older generation might view a traditional firm handshake with a man or a woman as too bold or aggressive. Old standards dictated that people with the highest level of authority should extend their hands first and others should wait for this gesture.*

In today's world, everyone shakes hands with each other. It's considered an extremely polite way to greet one another and is acceptable in almost every social situation. In business, however, shaking hands is critical.

It makes an immediate impression and symbolizes warmth and trust. The following article was written years ago for exhibitors at a trade show (back in the day when the world had something called the telephone booth, remember those?), but it applies to everyone. The data suggests that just this small simple gesture can make a world of difference.

Put it There

By Dr. Allen Konopacki

In an age where the word communication conjures up images of phone lines and video screens, a trade show seems like the one place where meeting in person is still an important concept.

The success of the trade show industry proves that even in a world where technology reigns supreme, nothing is as effective as face-to-face contact. Yet, a new study suggests that exhibitors are leaving out a key element for making in-person meetings valuable: the handshake. The study, conducted by the Incomm Center for Trade Show Research, found that in theory, practice, and fact, a little shake of the hand goes a long way toward giving your booth a boost.

Theory

Why do handshakes matter? They create warmth, trust, and a sense of an immediate mutual relationship. They are also a great way to make your exhibit stand out from the others. People tend to remember a person who greets them with a handshake more than those who don't, and they'll be more likely to return to that person's booth because they felt welcome.

The first time you greet someone is critical because a relationship is usually established in the first four seconds of contact. There's an art to working trade shows successfully, and using a handshake can create a positive impression that can eventually win you sales.

Practice

To better understand the importance of handshakes, the following experiment was conducted for the study. A group of students left a quarter in a public phone booth. After strangers used the phone and took the coin, one of the students walked up to ask if they had seen the quarter. Of the roughly seventy-five people who were approached, over forty lied, saying that they had never seen the twenty-five cents they had pocketed.

The experiment was then tried with another group of seventy-five strangers, with the difference being that the student greeted the person with a quick handshake and an introduction, then asked if the quarter had been spotted. Of this group, the number of people who fibbed dropped to eighteen of the seventy-five.

The conclusion was simple: handshakes create a higher degree of intimacy and trust within a matter of seconds. In fact, the gesture carries perhaps more weight than ever because so many face-to-face encounters have been replaced by phone calls, faxes, and e-mail. A handshake is perceived as being reserved for personal attention.

Fact

Examples are all fine and good, but the evidence that handshakes have an actual effect is based on hard numbers. Here are the industry facts: Only 8 percent of exhibit sales representatives greet visitors at a trade show exhibit with a handshake. Even worse, the typical greetings used by salespeople, such as "Can I answer any questions?" or "May I help you?" are impersonal, and thus reduce comfort and trust.

When greeted with a handshake, 76 percent of individuals respond by being more open, friendly, and honest. Salespeople who shake hands with a prospect or customer are twice as likely to be remembered compared to those salespeople who don't shake hands. In short, handshakes build a higher degree of interaction and memorability.

The previous article was reprinted with permission from Trade Show Ideas, a publication of the Trade Show Exhibitors Association, McCormick Place, 2301 South Lake Shore Drive, Suite 1005, Chicago, Illinois 60616; www.tsea.org.

How Exactly Do You Shake Hands?

Since the handshake is considered by many to be a symbol of trust, friendship, and approachability, I think it's critical that you learn the proper way to shake someone's hand. Although I think it's unnecessary to explain the basic technique (I'm sure you all know how to shake someone's hand!), I do have a few thoughts:

Keep it dry.

Your hands should be warm and dry. There is nothing worse than shaking a sweaty hand. If the other person's hand was sweaty, please do not wipe your hands on your pants to dry them off because that would be considered extremely rude.

Stand up.

Always stand up when you shake someone's hand, unless, of course, you are both sitting down.

Make eye contact.

Look the person directly in the eye and shake his or her hand with a firm grip while offering a verbal greeting.

Not too tight, please.

For the men, please make sure that you don't squeeze too hard because if you do, you'll break the other person's hand or bring tears to the person's eyes. It's happened to me more times than I can count, and I often have to discreetly shake my hand to get the blood circulating again.

Of course, if you squeeze too hard, people might think you're either being aggressive or hostile toward them because it feels like you're trying to break their hand.

After I wrote that last paragraph, I sat back in my chair and wondered what men thought when it happened to them? Did it happen to them? So I went downstairs and asked my husband Ron what goes through his mind when a man shakes his hand too hard. He looked up from the newspaper he was reading and said simply, "I think he's a jerk."

Enough said.

Firm it up.

For the ladies, please don't give me a limp fish handshake. I'm sure you've all received one of these. It's a soft handshake where the individual doesn't squeeze your hand at all.

No pumping.

My arm is not a water spout, so please don't pump it. If you must, then two short pumps of the arm are all you need. Your forearm (your arm from your elbow to your hand) should be the only thing moving up and down. Shake the hand a few times then release your hand completely.

Release the hand quickly.

Please don't hold onto the person's hand for too long. You should only hold onto the hand for three to four seconds for a business handshake. A longer handshake is really only used for close friends.

No touching.

Don't put your hand on their shoulder, or any other part of their body for that matter, as you'll be invading their personal space. Invading someone's personal space is socially unacceptable in the United States.

Never reject someone offering their hand.

It's considered extremely rude to reject a handshake so please don't. In fact, if you are a concierge, you should always shake someone's hand. Now I completely understand that there will be some situations where that is not possible, that's fine. Just shake hands whenever you can.

What about germs?

If you are worried about the germs you might catch from shaking another person's hand (please don't laugh, I get asked about this all the time), just carry a small bottle of hand sanitizer with you. After you have shaken hands and the person has walked away from you, you can discreetly sanitize your hands. Doing this right in front of the other person would be extremely rude.

Chapter Six

Professional Image

Key to Excellence:

Always dress for success.

You are the image of your company, so you should dress appropriately at all times. If you leave a lasting impression, then both you and your company will be remembered. I suggest that you make that first impression a lasting one because you may not get a second chance. In fact, more than half of our first impressions are based on appearance.

According to Angie Michael, author of *Best Impressions in Hospitality and Business Casual Made Easy*, "Professional dress is more than our public skin. It is a language. Clothing defines and describes us to the world."

Furthermore, Michael goes on to say that "your employees are the ambassadors of your organization. They are there in the front lines representing your company, and the way they are perceived determines how your organization is perceived by customers, the community, and the marketplace."

She's right. Your front desk employees are absolutely the most important people in your company, and their appearance is critical. That being said, what do you think is the first thing someone's going to notice when they're shaking your hand?

Your smile?

Possibly.

Your clothing and how you dress?

Absolutely.

Therefore, proper clothing is a must. I can't stress this enough because you want them to remember you and your business, not what you wore because it was so outrageous.

Here's an example: I remember a salesperson who showed up for a meeting with me wearing a tight low-cut shirt and an extremely short skirt. I have no memory of what she was trying to sell me, nor do I remember what our conversation was about. I only remember her clothes and how she kept yanking at her shirt to pull it up. I'm absolutely positive that this was not the impression she intended to leave me with.

According to Diana Pemberton-Sikes, author of the book *Wardrobe Magic*, "Dressing for success isn't about having the 'right' suit, the 'right' watch, or the 'right' haircut; it's about dressing to successfully RELATE to people with whom you want to do business. It's about being a chameleon, about blending in. People want to associate with people like themselves. If you don't look enough like them in terms of dress, manner, or position, you'll be perceived as an outsider. They may never feel comfortable enough to learn anything more about you, let alone do business with you."

A few tips regarding your professional image:

Anything you wear should be clean, neat, and wrinkle-free.

Torn, dirty, or frayed clothing is unacceptable.

Your style of clothing depends on what service you are providing.

For example, if you were pitching a corporate client or real estate management company, then I would suggest suitable business attire. If, on the other hand, you are running around town, then I suggest pants and a collared shirt of some kind, perhaps with your company logo on it.

Stand up straight.

Good posture is the key.

SMILE!

Be confident.

Keep your nervous habits under control.

Nervous habits such as biting your nails, twisting your hair, and bouncing your knee up and down rapidly can ruin your professional image, so do the best you can to get those under control. Personally, if I'm talking to someone and his or her knee is twitching like a machine gun, I tend to pay attention to the knee and not what the person is saying. It's distracting.

Please do NOT chew gum. Nothing ruins a professional image more than someone snapping their gum while they're talking to you.

Here's an example. Just the other day I went to the drive-through window to make a deposit. The teller's voice was pleasant and he said all the right things, but when I looked out my car window at him, he was standing there chewing a piece of gum with his mouth open. All I could do was shake my head. The last thing I need to see is food in someone's mouth. Here's the bottom line: if you're going to chew gum (and you shouldn't when you're at work), at least chew with your mouth closed.

Be clean and fresh.

I shouldn't have to tell you that you need to shower, be clean, use deodorant, and have good breath. Also, please try and keep your perfume or cologne to a minimum because if I can smell you before you enter the room, then you're wearing too much.

Dress for success!

Conservative and classic clothing is always a good choice. If you work for a company, then I suggest that you take a look at what your supervisor and coworkers are wearing. If they wear business suits, so should you. If they're wearing golf shirts and khaki shorts, then that's what you should wear.

How do you want people to see you? Do you want them to see a serious professional who is ready to meet clients or customers? Then you must dress that way. You want your boss to notice the great work you're doing, not what you're wearing.

If it's "dress down Friday" and you're wearing shorts, then they should be long enough to cover all the appropriate body parts. The shorts should be middle-fingertip length when your arms are relaxed.

Also, please don't wear bare midriff shirts, strapless shirts, undergarments worn as outer garments, sagging pants, or see-through clothing of any kind.

Don't dress like you are going out to a bar for the evening. Tight clothes, short skirts, sequins, and muscle T-shirts should be left in your closet at home. Your party clothes should NOT be worn to the office.

Always dress for success because you just never know who you will run into.

It's All about Good Customer Service

An Interview with Erica Davis
The Ambassador's Touch, Inc.

Ms. Davis is currently the CEO of The Ambassador's Touch, Inc. She has been in the hospitality industry for more than ten years.

When you are training your staff to be concierges, what do you teach them? How do you teach them to act?

One of the first things that we teach them is that when you come in the door, whatever problems you are experiencing in your personal life be it relationships, medical problems, having trouble with your children, whatever, you leave those problems at the front door. They do not come inside with you because once you step inside those doors, your focus should be 100 percent on the residents or the employees that you are there to serve.

You give 110 percent every time. If someone is asking for directions to a bank from the building, a front desk clerk is going to print out directions and say "here you go." A concierge is going to print out the directions, pinpoint where you are now on the map, and draw the route to where you are trying to get to. A concierge will take it one step further. It's the same thing for restaurants. We've created a menu book for area restaurants. A front desk clerk will just hand guests the book to look at. A concierge is going to take the book and ask them what they are looking for. Takeout? Delivery? What type of cuisine would you like? Then the concierge will present the guests with options. Once they choose, the concierge will ask: "Would you like me to make a reservation for you?" or "Would you like me to call the order in and have it delivered to your door?" That's a concierge.

We teach them to go one step further.

While at the desk, their first priority is the tenant. If there are no tenants in the lobby, then they are required to do research. We have rolodexes on the desk, and they should be filled with information on restaurants, pet sitting companies, things like that. If you're not filling that in, then you're not doing your job. If they don't know the area well, then they research the area when the lobby is quiet. If you have nothing to do, then you should be researching.

The front desk is a professional desk. Personal items are not to be kept out. Your cell phone, purse, cups of coffee, water should all be under the desk. No eating; take it to the back. When someone comes through the front door, you don't wait for them to come to you, you greet them immediately, "Good morning, sir/ma'am." The same thing applies when they are leaving the building, "Have a good day sir/ma'am." Plus, they address clients by "sir" and "ma'am," or their surname. Never call clients by their first name. If they insist on the first name, then it's "Miss Erica."

You should never say "no" or "I don't know." These words should not be in your vocabulary. Instead, you should say, "I will find this information for you and will get back to you within thirty minutes."

You have to smile, be nice each and every time, and always take it one step further. It's all about good customer service.

Ms. Davis can be reached via her Web site at www.ambassadorstouch. com.

**The most important thing in communication
is to hear what isn't being said.**

— Peter F. Drucker

Chapter 7

Body Language and Nonverbal Communication

Key to Excellence:

Think, and be prepared for anything.

Have you ever walked up to someone and immediately noticed that he was angry? How did you know? Was it something he said or was it his body language? Most likely, it was his body language talking to you.

Here in the United States, the spoken word is the most important way we communicate with each other. However, in many other countries nonverbal communication (or body language) is often considered even more important.

According to a study by Albert Mehrabian on how people decide whether they like one another, it was discovered that only 7 percent based their decisions on the spoken word, 38 percent decided based on the tone of voice, and 55 percent based their decisions on body language. This clearly shows that nonverbal communication is an important part of communication and is one of the major ways we talk to each other. It is one of the most reliable indicators of what people think about you.

I think it's vital that you be aware of someone's body language as it will help you to understand that person's state of mind. You also should be aware of your own body language and how it may or may not match what your words are saying.

How about e-mail? That's a communication tool that is used by millions of people around the world. I find e-mail frustrating because words can be misinterpreted. If I can't read your body language, or listen to the tone of your voice, it's hard to know if you are angry or just joking around. That's why people use the word "LOL" so often in their e-mails and text messages. (For those who don't know, that means "laugh out loud".) Reading body language, therefore, is an important communication tool.

There Is No Such Thing as a Second Impression

Remember, there is no such thing as a second impression, so make your first impression a good one. With that in mind, here are some of my recommendations.

Smile!

I've said this a few times in this book, and I'm going to repeat it here again because it's so incredibly important. Smiling is contagious, so spread it around as much as possible. When someone grins at you, it's almost impossible not to smile back.

Shake their hand.

I've already addressed this issue in a previous chapter, but it bears repeating here. A handshake creates an instant feeling of warmth and trust. A firm handshake shows that you are confident and strong. Look people directly in the eye when you are shaking their hand as this will build their trust. If someone is constantly looking away from you and won't look you in the eyes, it might mean that the person is hiding something from you.

Don't fidget.

If you are wringing your hands or fidgeting, people will notice and will wonder what you are worried about. You need to appear calm and relaxed.

Be aware of signs that someone is not telling the whole truth.

If people are touching their eyes, nose, or ears a lot, or they're rubbing their hands together, then they might not be telling you the whole truth. These are body language tip-offs. They may also look away from you frequently and have trouble making eye contact.

Create the impression that you are open and interested.

Don't stand with your arms crossed over your chest as that makes you look closed and defensive. You want to appear open, warm, and friendly. Also, people who are interested in something tend to lean forward a bit when they are listening and/or speaking. So my advice is to lean forward slightly, tilt your head a little to one side, and remember to make eye contact.

Put others at ease and mirror what they are (and are not) doing.

For example, if the person seems to be a serious and conservative person, I would mirror that behavior by sitting up straight and talking in a conservative manner. I like to make people laugh in my workshops, but I can certainly teach the information straight when I have to. If they are serious, then so am I. This way my attendees are more comfortable.

Pay attention to what they are doing.

For example, if they are tapping their fingers on the table, it could mean that they are impatient for you to be finished. If they are rubbing their eyes a lot, it could mean they are tired, of course, but it could also mean they don't believe you.

Try nodding your head when you agree with what they are saying; it's the universal signal of agreement.

Here's something interesting: Not only is nodding your head a universal sign of agreement, but it might also be a way to communicate your own thoughts and feelings to yourself. According to a study done at Ohio State University by Richard Petty and Pablo Brinol, "Nodding your head up and down is, in effect, telling yourself that you have confidence in your own thoughts—whether those thoughts are positive or negative. Shaking your head from side to side does the opposite: its gives people less confidence in their own thoughts."

Look for signs of boredom. If they're bored with your conversation, their body language will tell you.

A bored person will find other things to do while you're talking to him. Most likely, he'll doodle on a piece of paper, look at his watch, or even tap his foot. A bored person is constantly doing something. If you see the person is bored, it's time to end the conversation fast and let him go.

Now this is all well and good, but please make sure you don't judge people based on one thing alone. For example, I stand with my arms crossed quite a bit, but it doesn't mean that I'm being defensive; it usually means I'm cold. It might also mean that I have a stain on my shirt. As I said, never jump to conclusions based on one behavior.

A good concierge needs to do three things when you are talking to people. You need to listen to their words, pay attention to their body language, and trust what your intuition is telling you because it's usually right.

Take Their Request, and Then Go Above and Beyond It

An Interview with Leslie O. Graham
Washington , D.C.

Mr. Graham worked as the head concierge for the Ritz Carlton Resort in St. Thomas, U.S. Virgin Islands, and is currently working as a concierge in Washington, DC. He is also the founder of Ambassador Concierge (www.ambassadorconciergellc.com).

When you are teaching people to be a concierge, what do you tell them? What are your top tips?

The first thing I tell my concierges is to listen to the guests. Listen to their needs and their concerns. Then, after you've listened to their needs and concerns, put yourself in their place and see how you would want to be served. Then you act upon it. Always do your very best and never make them a promise you can't keep.

I never know how I'm going to talk to guests until I meet them. Then I talk to them like I've known them forever. I also have a good sense of humor. One guest told me the other day, "I remember you, you're the guy with the great sense of humor!" They always remember me because of how I make them feel. I can turn a sad face into a smile every time using words and facial expressions. I never turn anyone away; I assist everyone, regardless of who they are, even if the call was for another department. I take it upon myself to solve the guests' problems and meet their needs.

I try and tell my employees to act like you are the visitor. Put yourself in their place. If you are going somewhere and went to a concierge, how would you want to be treated? Be knowledgeable about the area and the products you recommend, like restaurants and boat trips for example. Take trips; go to restaurants; don't tell them you're from the Ritz Carlton; see what kind of service they have. Pay attention to what the staff does and how they react to you. This way you can tell your clients. I like service. I like to be waited on, and I like to be spoken to and have conversations with people. I like attention. This is how I treat people. One thing I hate is ad-libbing—you've never been to the restaurant but you try and sell it to the guest anyway. Often, the guests then come back and say they didn't like it.

So you're approachable and have a positive outlook on life, and there is no such thing as "that's not my job."

Exactly. Everything is my job. You have to be warm and friendly and smile a lot. No matter what personal problems I might have at home, it's not brought to work. I don't just stay behind the desk. I come around from the desk and interact with the guests. They're people just like you and I. You should treat people like you would a guest in your home. That's how you get repeat business because we always go back to places that make us feel the best.

I tell my staff to treat all the guests like they are a VIPs. Everyone is a VIP! I treat everyone the same way. Even when I'm not at work and in the grocery store, I'm acting like I'm a concierge using the verbiage that I've learned over the years. It's how I like to be treated. Sometimes you walk up to the cash register, and the cashier's not smiling. I smile at her, and it makes her feel good.

For me, being a concierge is a life choice. It's all about the way you treat people. It's about creating a memorable experience for the guest. To use your term, it's about going above and beyond. Take their request, and then go above and beyond it. Go that extra step. Remember, if you show empowerment and good service, someone is going to notice you, and you'll find yourself moving up in the organization.

Quality service means never having to say, "That's not my job."

— James H. Donnelly, Jr.

Chapter 8

The Lobby and Front Desk Staff

Key to Excellence:

Be warm, friendly and approachable.

Who do you think the most important person is in the company?

Your CEO?

No.

The president of the company?

A good answer, but no.

It's your front desk staff. The people who are the first ones to greet the public are the most important people in the company. If clients get a bad first impression when they are greeted, then it sours their entire experience and might cause you to lose them as clients.

Therefore, it goes without saying that the receptionist, security guard, concierge, and anyone else who is on the front lines of a company needs to provide incredible customer service. They should be warm, friendly, accommodating, approachable, pleasant, and willing to go that extra mile for someone.

Here are some basics for those who work in lobbies or at front desks:

Smile.

Yes, I'm saying this again. Please smile.

Stand up.

When someone enters the lobby (or the room where you are working), please stand up and greet the person. If you're on the phone, or you just can't stand up for some reason, that's fine. Just stand up as much as you can. Also, please shake the person's hand whenever possible.

Greet people as they walk into the lobby, and then again when they leave.

A warm and friendly greeting with a smile on your face is perfect. Try and get to know people's names as fast as possible so that you can greet them by name the next time they come. Name recognition is one of the keys to being a truly great concierge.

If you are not good at remembering people's names, there are a few things you can try to help you. First, when you first meet someone, try and repeat his or her name over and over again in your mind. Repeating the word over and over as you look at the person's face will help you remember the name. I would also try and repeat the person's name in the first sentence:

Client: "Hello, Mr. Concierge. My name is Ted Jones."

You: "Hello, Mr. Jones, it's a pleasure to meet you."

If you just can't remember a name, do what I do and just admit it. I'm very adept at saying, "My apologies, I recognize your face but I just can't seem to recall your name." However, try and not do that more than once.

Never leave your desk. This is one of the biggest rules of the concierge industry.

In a hotel, concierges rarely leave their post. If they must leave their desk, many concierges put a clock on their desk that states what time they will return. However, if you tell clients that you'll be back in ten minutes, then please make sure that you are back in ten minutes. There is nothing more irritating than having to wait for someone to return.

I remember an experience at a music store trying to pick up some music for my son. When I arrived at the store, there was a sign posted that said the clerk would be back in ten minutes. As I turned to look for a place to sit, a woman standing behind me told me she'd already been waiting twenty minutes. Since she was clearly annoyed, I tried a little small talk to see if I could distract her and calm her down a bit. Unfortunately, it didn't work. When the clerk finally arrived, she let him have it with a verbal assault. He apologized and told her why he was late, but she didn't care because his tardiness had made her further late for another appointment. People don't want to hear your excuses when they're angry, and she was no exception.

The moral to this story? Never make a promise you can't keep.

Please do NOT eat at your desk.

Never eat at your desk. Period. There are no exceptions to this rule.

You may have a bottle of water on your desk, but only if it's discreet. I suggest that you place the bottle in a desk drawer or on the floor somewhere so it won't spill. You could also use an attractive coffee mug. I've seen some hotel concierges place their cup behind a bouquet of flowers so that clients can't see it when they walk up to the desk.

I suggest that you walk into any hotel and look at the concierge desk. Do you see any food, water, or coffee cups on it? No? Enough said.

Keep your desk and/or work station neat and tidy.

Your desk should be neat. Clients shouldn't see huge stacks of paper, funny comics taped to the side of the computer, and stuffed animals by the pencil holder.

Do <u>NOT</u> use your cell phone.

A cell phone screams that you are on a personal phone call, so please keep your phone discreetly hidden. If it rings and you are talking to someone, please do your best to NOT look at it to see who is calling. When I'm having a conversation with someone, I find it incredibly irritating when the person interrupts our conversation to glance at his or her cell phone to see who is calling. Put your cell phone ringer on either vibrate or low so that your clients can't hear it. If you must take the call, then simply walk outside the building and have your conversation there. Using a cell phone or texting people from your desk is never appropriate.

Stay busy.

If there is no one in the lobby, what do you do? Many companies will allow you to read as long as you are discreet about it. If you choose to read, then please make sure that the newspaper is lying flat on the desk so clients can't see it when they walk in. Other companies want you to stay busy by doing research on the Internet, finding local vendors and restaurants, and discovering what events are happening around town that week. Both are fine as long as you look up as soon as someone approaches your desk and give the client your immediate attention.

Help clients promptly.

This is important and can never be repeated too often:

Do not allow clients to stand in front of you for more than a few seconds before you acknowledge that you've seen them and will be with them momentarily.

To help you, the following are a few techniques that concierges use when they are on the phone with one client and another client needs to be served:

1.   Smile, look a client in the eye, and nod your head slightly to indicate that you've seen him or her. Then please try and hang up the phone as soon as possible without being rude to either the person waiting or the one on the phone. You can also give waiting clients a "one minute" sign with your hand (please don't point in any way, as many will find that rude). Again, end the call as soon as possible.

2.   If more than a few minutes go by and the client is still standing in front of you waiting, ask the caller if you can place him or her on hold for a moment. Smile and greet the individual in front of you politely, apologize for making the person wait, and ask how you can help the person. If the client's request will take a while for you to answer, ask the client to wait just one more minute while you quickly finish your call.

3.   You can say, "I'll be on the phone for a few minutes more, would you mind waiting or would you like me to call you?"

A good rule of thumb here is to help the person who spoke to you first. If the phone rang first, then that client gets priority. You can then try some of the techniques that I listed above. However, if the person standing in front of you was first, then answer the phone and politely ask the caller if you can place him or her on hold for a minute. If it takes more than a moment, go back to the call and ask if you can call the client back or would the client like to keep holding.

Of course, there are dozens of other methods concierges are using around the country, but I think you get the idea here. The main key is this: the longer someone has to wait for you to acknowledge him or her, the bigger the chance that the client will simply walk away.

A few years back, my husband Ron and I went to a local national bank to open up a new account. We walked in and looked around for someone to help us, and when we found no one, we sat down on the couch in the lobby and waited for someone to serve us.

We waited and waited and waited.

We sat there for more than fifteen minutes, and no one approached us. Why did they think we were sitting there? For the fun of it? Because we liked the ambiance of the bank? So we left and went to the bank that was near our home.

As soon as we walked into the bank, we were greeted by a warm and friendly gentleman who immediately took us to an office. He then offered us something to drink and found someone to help us. The bank staff couldn't have been nicer, and we opened an account on the spot.

So if you don't want to lose the customer, then please don't let him or her sit or stand for more than a few seconds before you walk up and offer a greeting. At the very least, please acknowledge that you've seen the customer and will be with him or her in a minute. If you have several people waiting, then make sure you have a solid way of knowing who is next in line! Just put that fire out before it happens. You can also offer something for customers to do—magazines, newspapers, TV, radio— something to help them pass the time while they wait.

Ideally, I think you should have someone at the door greeting people. The greeter will greet customers at the door, offer refreshments, make sure that they know who is next in line, and then walk the person to the staff member they are waiting for—like the bank did in my example. Greeters can even engage customers in small talk to make the time go by faster. The more pleasant the waiting experience, the happier your customers will be.

Don't chat with co-workers; pay attention to customers.

Am I the only one who gets annoyed when the cashier is chatting with the bagger and completely ignoring me? If there is a customer in front of you, stop talking to your associate and pay attention to the customer and his or her needs. The customer comes first, no matter what.

Keep your promises to follow up.

If you promise to call clients back, then call them back. No exceptions. Plus, if you tell them you'll get back to them before five, call them at four. As I stated before, always underpromise and overdeliver. Over-the-top extraordinary customer service is the key to being a truly great concierge.

Never say "no." Everything is now your job.

The word "no" should be eliminated from your vocabulary. Please do not say:

"No, I can't do that for you."

Instead, try saying this:

"I don't provide those services. However if you give me your telephone number, I would be happy to find someone who can."

Or,

"Sir, our hotel is full tonight, but the hotel around the corner has availability." (Then offer to call your competitor and make a reservation if you want to go above and beyond!)

The moral here is that if you have to say no, then always provide the client with another option.

Take it up a notch.

Even if you get asked really stupid questions, you should always take the time to politely answer them. In fact, I would like you to not only answer them, but take it up a notch. Here's an example:

"When does the seven o'clock movie start?"

Rather than roll your eyes and laugh, take it up a notch by answering as follows:

"It starts at seven o'clock. However, it gets really crowded right before curtain time, so make sure you get here at least thirty minutes early. If you stand right under that tree over there, you'll be in good shape because that's where the line starts, and you should be one of the first ones in the theater."

Always go above and beyond.

Put yourself in your customer's shoes.

Sit in the lobby and pretend you are a customer. What do you see? How do you feel?

Is your lobby a place where customers will be waiting for a while? Then perhaps providing magazines or newspapers to peruse would be appropriate.

How about someplace for customers to sit?

Would complimentary coffee be appropriate, or a water cooler?

Is there a bowl of candy or something on the table?

Are there fresh flowers on the desk?

Is there a trash can readily available?

If you want your company to behave like a first-class concierge, then providing over-the-top details will help you get there. Sometimes it's the little things that make the biggest impression on people. As I've said before, people may not remember what you've done for them, but they will absolutely remember how you made them feel.

The Disney Institute sums it up well by saying, "Exceed expectations by paying attention to the details."

You Should Have a Can-Do Attitude

An Interview with Jill Suzanne Preis
Just Personal Service, LLC

Ms. Preis has worked in the events, hospitality, and personal service in-dustry for more than fifteen years. She is currently the owner of Just Per-sonal Service, LLC and JPS Events, offering concierge and event services to Midwest corporations and private clients.

If you were going to teach concierges, what would you tell them?

To be a good concierge, it's important that you smile and be ap-proachable. You need to be a genuine person and kind. Clients need to feel confident in you, and you need to feel like family to them. I try to stand up when people come into the lobby, and I'll come out from behind my desk, smile, and shake their hand. Be nice and genuine. You should have a can-do attitude—it's never can't.

One key thing is that you need to be there. Seeing your friendly face on a daily basis is critical. Also, knowing when people are in your lobby during busy times is the key to being available to them. When there is a lull in our lobby, that's when I do things that take me away from the desk. If I'm going to be out for a while, then I'll put a sign on the desk stating when I'll be back.

You should also be organized and keep your desk clean. Make sure all the magazines and reading material in the lobby are current. No dated issues. Keep it simple; don't put tons of stuff out unless you're sure you can keep everything current.

When clients ask for something, if I can't get it to them immediately, I'll ask if I can bring it up to them within the hour. Instead of me trying to fumble through and print things out, I think it wastes their time. If they're standing there and my computer doesn't work, I can't get a Web site up, or something happens, then they might think, "I could have done this on my own." It also makes me nervous knowing they're waiting for me to finish. I'd much rather put the information together in a nice way, attach a handwritten note, and take it up to them. This way I can give them my full attention.

You need to prioritize. If you can get a request done right away when it comes in, then do it. Things will hit you one after the other, and you might agree to get something to a client in ten minutes, and you'll get hit with five telephone calls in a row. So don't make promises you can't keep.

Another thing with lobbies is that people like to stay and talk. They'll open their mail by the desk and chat. I always encourage them to open their mail and sit in one of the spaces in the reception area, just not at my desk. If another resident comes in while I'm chatting with someone casually, then I can go back to the desk and sit and talk to the resident that needs help.

You also need to learn about the residents as fast as you can. I know everyone in the building and read their profiles when I first started. You learn their likes and dislikes very quickly. That's the name of the game. It's what we do. I ask questions to get to know them better rather than waiting for them to come to me. You really need to go to your clients, and they'll tell you right away whether they're interested or not. You need to be proactive.

To read more about Ms. Preis, visit her Web site at
www.justpersonalservice.com.

**The test of good manners
is to be patient with bad ones.**

— Gabirol (Solomon ben Yehuda ibn Gabirol),
The Choice of Pearls

Chapter 9

Communications Skills

Key to Excellence:

Communicating well is critical.

A while back, I received an e-mail from a potential corporate client. Since I had a meeting that would last most of the day, I decided it would be quicker to just simply pick up the phone and call him. So I placed the call and waited for him to answer. On the fifth ring, someone picked up the phone and said nothing. In fact, all I heard was breathing.

Now, please, correct me if I'm wrong, but shouldn't you say something into the phone when you pick it up? Like a simple hello perhaps?

Nothing.

So I immediately said, "Hello, is this Mr. Smith?"

He replied with a curt "yes" and nothing more. I politely identified myself, and the conversation began.

Here's my advice: Please don't do that. When you answer the phone, it's customary to do something more than just breathe into it.

The telephone is critically important as it's often the first contact you have with someone. So answering it in a professional manner is key. If you have a home office and your children are home, I would also urge you to keep them quiet when you answer your phone. It's hard to be professional when your children are screaming in the background. Also, your credibility will sink like a stone if your child answers the phone, which happened to me once years ago. My oldest son (who was about eight or nine at the time) answered the phone, took a message, and then gave it to me when he saw me later. When I returned the call, the woman immediately said, "Now before you say anything to me at all, I have to tell you that your son did an excellent job and you shouldn't yell at him." Relieved beyond belief, I thanked her and the conversation began.

After I finished the call, I searched out my son to apologize, because, of course, I had already yelled at him. It's now many years later, and my son is in high school. This past summer, he worked in my office as my assistant. When the phone rang on his first day, he just looked at me and smiled. Remembering that day so long ago, he told me that the phone was ringing and quietly went back to work.

Telephone Etiquette

Here are a few tips to help you polish your telephone etiquette:

Answer the phone quickly and not with speakerphone.

Don't let it go past the third ring if you can avoid it.

Speaker phones tend to give callers the impression that you're not giving them your full attention. Plus, I always wonder who else is sitting in the room listening to our conversation. Ask permission to put someone on speaker before doing so.

Have a good opening and identify yourself.

When you answer the phone, give your name and the name of the company. For example: "Good morning, Triangle Concierge, this is Katharine. May I help you?"

Be warm and friendly when you answer the phone.

Your voice is the first impression the caller has of your company, so make it a good one. Leave your foul mood at home.

Smile when you're speaking to clients.

People can tell when you're smiling into the phone, and when you're not. So smile!

Slow down when leaving a voice message.

If you are the one leaving a message on someone's voice mail, please say your name and telephone number SLOWLY. I had to listen to a message four times the other day because the woman spoke so fast I couldn't get the number. Slow down, people.

Please don't eat or drink when you're on the phone with someone.

There is nothing more annoying than listening to someone swallowing or crunching on the phone.

Don't tell the caller you "don't know."

Instead, I advise you to say, "Let me find that out for you, and I'll call you back before the end of the day."

Don't do your research while the customer is on the phone or standing right in front of you.

If the person is standing in front of you, and you know it will take only a few seconds to get an answer, then say:

"I would be happy to do that for you. It will take me a few moments to get that information, so if you wouldn't mind waiting a minute, I'll get the answer for you right now."

If you think it might take longer than a minute, then you have a few choices depending on the situation:

    1. "I would be happy to do that for you. It will take me a few moments to get that information. May I please put you on hold?"

2. "I would be happy to do that for you. It will take me a few moments to get that information, so is there a phone number where I can reach you? It shouldn't take longer than ___ minutes."

3. "This is going to take me a few minutes to research. May I please put you on hold or would you prefer for me to call you right back?" If the answer is "yes, you may put me on hold," then you should ask for a telephone number "just in case we get disconnected." The client might be on a cell phone, and the call might accidently be dropped.

Please remember, if the client is on the telephone, and you think you can get the answer in under a minute, then you can do your research while the client is listening to you. However, if you think it will take more than a minute, then please don't keep the client hanging on the line. Ask if you can put him or her on hold and then do your research.

Now why would I tell you to do that?

If the research takes more than a minute, then it's much more professional to call the client back or place the client on hold. If you have to search for the answer for a while, you're not going to be able to help talking to your client. In fact, you might even accidently say things like "Let me check the company's Web site," or "Umm, ahhh, hold on a minute and let me Google that."

Now you have a client who is wondering why she didn't just do that herself, which is one of the reasons why your client should never know where you got the information. All the client needs to know is that you got the information she wanted fast, and you gave her outstanding service.

Also, please do not allow your client to stay on hold for more than a minute. After a minute, go back to the client and apologize for making her wait. Then please ask if she would like to continue to hold or would she prefer that you call her back.

Cut down the "umms" and "ahhs" as much as possible.

Listen to what the client is saying so you get it right. You should be doing more listening and little talking. I also suggest that you repeat back the request and other vital information (such as the client's credit card information and address) to make sure that you heard everything correctly.

NEVER call the client by his or her first name!

I'll say this once again because I think it's so important. Please address your client as Mr. Smith, Mrs. Smith, ma'am, or sir.

Take the time to ask clients how they spell their name.

Never, ever, assume that you know how to spell someone's name. Take my name for example. There are perhaps ten different ways to spell "Katharine," and mine is the rarest. How about the name Sara? Or do you spell it Sarah? How about Ann? Or is it Anne? Take the time to ask, no matter how simple the name.

Please do NOT say "you're welcome" ever again.

I understand that we were all taught to say, "You're welcome," but I would prefer that you say, "It was my pleasure." The reason for this is that it will set you apart from everyone else. When was the last time you heard someone say, "It was my pleasure" to you? Those four little words will set you above and beyond the rest.

Have a good closing.

"May I help you with anything else today?" Then, if they don't wish you to do anything further, close with a "thank you for calling ABC Company. Have a great day."

Let's Talk Voice Mail

I had to make a lot of phone calls a while back, and although I did reach a few people, I also listened to quite a few voice mail messages. After listening to dozens of them, I have a few suggestions.

One of the first messages I listened to was actually the most irritating of them all. No disrespect intended, but the caller spoke so slowly that I felt like she was talking down to me, a feeling that you don't want your clients to have when they call you. I suspect this person is losing business because people today just don't have the time to wait.

Another person didn't identify himself or his company, so it was hard to know if I reached the correct phone number. In fact, several people didn't even bother to set up their voice mail; a computer answered the phone in one of those "one size fits all" voice messages.

Also, please don't make the message too long. One message went on and on about the company's fax number, its other companies, whose box was which and whatnot. By the end of the message I had almost forgotten what I called for. Anyone else would have simply hung up before the end of the message.

Here's my favorite: one voice mail had a short and sweet message that said, "We cannot accept your call; please leave a message."

Accept? Really? Am I unacceptable? It was a poor choice of words.

How about the machine that disconnected me not one, not two, but three times! It also had a ninety-second message (which was really an advertisement for the business) that you had to listen to each time. I kept trying, but most people won't. You'll lose the client.

Then there were the people who spoke in a monotone voice. Their voice had no inflection, no emotion, nothing. I was left with the feeling that they didn't care if I called or not, and, not surprisingly, not one of them returned my call.

In fact, out of all the calls I made, few replied back. Perhaps it's due to the fact that I'm not a paying client, or maybe they were too busy. The reason doesn't matter because each and every call should be answered within twenty-four hours. Good customer service is a twenty-four-hour job and should be practiced with absolutely everyone. There are no exceptions.

Return voice mails (and e-mails) FAST!

I return everyone's call and e-mail lightning fast. Even when I'm on the road, everyone gets a response. Even if it's only to let them know that I'm on the road and will answer them in a few days. In fact, this simple thing has done more for growing my business than almost anything else I've done. If you want to practice outstanding customer service, then start by respecting your clients' time and answering them in twenty-four hours or less.

Here are a few suggestions to follow when creating your voice mail recording:

Keep your message to between fifteen and twenty-five seconds in length.

Any longer, and the caller will simply hang up. It should be short and concise. Please remember to give your name and company so the caller will know he or she dialed the right number.

Be positive.

You should sound like you really want to talk to people, that their message is important to you. If you talk in a monotone, do you really think people are going to want to use your services? Possibly not, because your voice is telling them that you really don't care and would much rather be somewhere else.

Talk as you would normally.

Don't talk too slowly because it doesn't sound normal. I understand that you are trying to speak clearly so that the caller can understand the message, but too slow is ridiculous and you could possibly lose clients.

Stay current.

If you leave a message that says you'll be out of the office until the first of the month, and I call on the fifth and get the same message, that's not good. Please remember to update your voice mail message as soon as you return.

Be careful with the music.

Please don't add background music—it's distracting.

Mind your manners.

Say please and thank you. Don't forget your manners.

Additional information is fine.

I would also quickly give callers your Web site address so they can find more information online. If you want to give them a short summary of your business, that's fine. Just don't do it on the main message—make it an option that they can choose. For example, "Press 1 to hear about our company, press 2 to reach Jane, press 3 for our fax number and directions to our company."

Written Communication

This book would not be complete if I didn't mention written communication skills. A letter (or e-mail) will be taken much more seriously if it's written well than one that is not. How would you write a letter to a political leader? How about the CEO of a company, or the principal of your school? Your letter should be clear and concise. There are hundreds of websites, books, software, and templates that will help you write an effective business letter, so I won't go into a great detail. However, I do have some advice because to be an outstanding concierge you must act professionally and have excellent communication skills.

Write in a formal style

Emails are written in a conversational style while business letters are more formal. So write your letters as if you are writing to the President of the United States. You should apply the general rules for writing a formal letter and there are plenty of examples of these in books and on the internet. You should use formal and polite language. Slang words are inappropriate, and remember to be courteous.

Use good quality paper

Your business letter should be written on bond paper that weighs at least 24 pounds. Bond paper comes in several different finishes which will add some texture to your letterhead. Nice paper stock can give the impression that you have a successful company that people want to do business with. If you have a company logo, add it to your letterhead design. Don't forget to include the pertinent information such as your company name, address, telephone number, fax number, email and website address. Don't forget the matching envelopes!

Handwritten notes

Don't forget the power of a handwritten thank you note! It's a symbol of outstanding customer service. Make sure that your handwriting is legible, and you use some good stationary.

Proofread, proofread, proofread!!

Business letters are the first impression that you make on someone, so make it a good one and proofread your work! Run the document through a spelling and grammar check before you print it. You should use proper grammar and complete sentences. Ask someone else to look it over. We all miss mistakes.

Email Correspondence

Style

Your email should be clear, consistent and courteous. As a general rule, business letters should be formal in style. Even if you know the person, you should still maintain some formality as it might be read by more than one person in their office.

Don't type in CAPS!

Typing in all capital letters in an email means that you are shouting.

Avoid using slang words and IM text

Avoid using words that you use in your IM messages. Words such as LOL (for laugh outloud) and "ur" (for your) should never be used in an email. They are unprofessional and do not give a good impression of your business.

Run it through a spell check

Always, and I mean always, run your letter or email through a spell and grammar check before you send it. Also, please double check the person's name and make sure you are spelling both their name and company correctly.

Don't write one long paragraph

Over the years, I've received many emails that are one big paragraph. Please don't do that. Use paragraphs. They make it easier to read the text and organize the different topics.

Have a proper closing

Don't just write your name at the bottom. Use words such as sincerely, warm regards, kind regards, regards, or cordially. Plus, if this is a business letter on letterhead, then you should personally sign it in ink at the bottom. In emails, I use this same philosophy by signing it in the following manner …

Warm regards,

Katharine

Katharine C. Giovanni
President and Cofounder
Triangle Concierge, Inc.
Tel: 919-453-2850
Email: kgiovanni@triangleconcierge.com
Websites: www.triangleconcierge.com
www.katharinegiovannicom
www.ICEAWeb.org

When sending an email, always think before you send it

Don't just hit the "send" key when you're done typing. Read it first. Are you sending it to the correct person or did you hit the "reply all" key by accident? There is nothing worse than sending out an email to the wrong person. Furthermore, NEVER ever send an email when you're angry! Write the email and then wait at least 24 hours before you send it. Is your email worded correctly? Does it convey the right information? Read the entire email before you send it to make sure that there are no mistakes.

Everyone Who Works in Front of the Public Should Be Warm, Friendly, and Honest

An Interview with Carla Mandell, Co-Founder International Concierge and Errand Association

Why is effective communication so important to a concierge?

Returning e-mails and telephone calls is one of the quickest ways to get business, especially if you return them fast. This is especially true with your current clients. In today's electronic world, a fast re-turn telephone call from a live person is critical. Plus, if you don't return it fast, you risk losing the client because the client will move on to someone else. Good service is the key. Even having those "out of office" notices on your phone (and in an auto-responder for your e-mail), as annoying as they are, at least tells callers that you're out serving clients and will get back to them within twenty-four hours. Of course, you must then follow through and answer them within twenty-four hours or less. If you take longer than that, the potential client will move on. Most people don't plan their life that far in ad-vance; they need things done right away.

When the client is standing in front of you, it's easy to do his or her request right away. If the request is sent to you in an e-mail or left on your voice mail, it's easier to put it off and say, "I'll get to that later." Here's an example, if the media contacts me regarding the industry and asks me to put them in touch with a few of our mem-bers, I'm only going to give them the names of the ones whom I know will respond right away. The media has a deadline, so I need members who have a reputation for answering quickly. If I know a member doesn't respond quickly, then I don't refer them to the media. Even if they are the best concierge in the world, the person

I'm speaking with needs an answer immediately, so I only give the names of people I can rely on to answer fast.

How do you write an effective professional e-mail?

I would write it like you would write a letter to the president. Think of how you would write a formal letter to the president of the United States, the mayor of your town, or the principal of your school. It's the same language you would use in a term paper for high school or a thesis in college.

What advice do you have for my readers?

Everyone who works in front of the public should be warm, friendly, and honest. It's crucial that you know your product and do your research so that you can answer any question you might get. Also, please don't have a personal conversation with your colleague if you have a customer standing in front of you. I can't tell you how many times I've been standing at a customer service desk to return something, and the cashiers ignore me because they're talking to each other about what they're wearing and where they're going that night. You need to focus on the customer because that's the quickest way to get people to return to your store. If you know that you're going to get excellent service when you go to a particular store, and you know that the staff is approachable, focused on the customer, will get you in and out quickly, and know what they are talking about, you're going to go to that store all the time.

I agree. There have been studies done that state that people will drive twice as far, and even endure less than satisfactory food, if they know they're going to get good service.

Yes! I have family that will drive across the state line because they prefer that chain restaurant over the one that is closer to us. Good customer service is the key.

If you want to learn how to act like a concierge, then you need to listen carefully to what people want, not what you think they want. You also need to check your ego at the door because, remember, it's all about them. That's my number one key: it's all about them. How do you make it about them? You listen to them, respond to everything quickly and clearly, and be honest, warm, and friendly. That's the secret.

Mrs. Mandell can be reached through ICEA's Web site: www.ICEAWeb.org.

Chapter 10

Yes, There are Rude Customers

Key to Excellence:

Treat people as you would like to be treated.

I was sitting in the airport waiting for my flight to board, when the woman sitting next to me struck up a conversation. After a few minutes, we got onto the topic of customer service. She then proceeded to tell me an interesting story about her father.

Apparently he wasn't a nice man, and when he developed cancer, he didn't get any nicer. She said it was amazing because her father could be as nasty as anything but the doctors and nurses never paid attention and were always lovely to him. She then told me that every year at Christmas he would send a gift to the doctor's office as a thank you present. You see, he never forgot how nice they were to him, and he was grateful.

As Mike Wall said earlier in this book, never take people's anger personally, as they might just be having a really bad day or under some serious stress. Deep down, like the grouchy patient, they will appreciate you and will remember that you were nice to them.

Look at it this way—you just don't know what kind of day they've had, or how much stress they are under. So make your words count as they might be the only nice ones the person hears that day.

So how do you treat customers, even if they're rude to you?

You should respond, not react.

When you respond, you think before you speak. When you react, you speak before you think. It's an emotional reaction. When someone is being rude to you, I want you to think first. You can't change what happened, but you can change how you react to it. If you have to, give yourself time to collect yourself—count to three, five, or even ten. This will allow the reactionary part of you to relax so that you can make the appropriate response.

Treat people like you would want to be treated.

Put yourself in their shoes. How would you want to be treated? I'll say it again—just be nice.

Provide flawless service.

You want the service you provide to be seamless. In other words, it should be flawless and smooth. Plus, it should go above and beyond anything the client has ever experienced.

Provide trustworthy service.

Trust is the hallmark of the concierge industry. Your clients and customers need to be able to trust you 100 percent. Trust is the foundation of all relationships, whether personal or business.

Be resourceful.

You should be resourceful and able to find anything, anywhere, anytime, for anyone. It goes without saying that you should never say "no." Always exceed your clients' expectations.

What to Do When the Client Is Unhappy with Your Service

At some point, you are going to have to handle an unhappy client. Don't worry; it happens to all of us. Remember, if you irritate one client, he'll tell one hundred people about his bad experience, but if you handle the situation right, then he will tell ten people how wonderful your company is. This is why it is so important to maintain a warm and positive relationship with all your clients.

When the customer does have a complaint, he or she needs to know four things.

1. That you've heard them.
2. That you've understood what they said.
3. That you care about their complaint.
4. That you're going to fix it immediately.

Listen.

Don't interrupt. Let them talk it out. We all want people to pay attention to us in this "it's all about me" world that we live in, so pay attention to them and listen. Let them vent their anger and frustration. Quite often, just letting them vent is enough to diffuse the situation because it makes them feel better.

Ask questions.

Your first priority is to figure out what the problem is, so ask questions. Clarity is the key here. It also shows that you really care about solving their problem. You want to make them feel appreciated and important. Also, use their name when you are talking to them. Please don't use words such as "Here's where you are wrong." Instead just agree with them and say things like, "I see" or "I'm so sorry that happened to you."

Apologize.

You don't want them to think you're giving them a "company policy" answer. Personalize your response and make them feel special. If they are standing in front of you, then walk over to them, look them in the eyes, and really listen to their problem. Then, immediately let them know that you completely understand their frustration and how upset they must be. Tell them how sorry you are that this happened to them. Tell them that you want to help solve their problem and will do everything possible to help them. The most important point here is to always apologize to the client.

Empathize.

Did you notice that I used the word empathize? Why didn't I tell you that you must sympathize? Here's why: if you don't have direct personal experience with a situation, then you can't sympathize.

When my mother died in 1990, if someone had come up to me and said, "I'm so sorry; I completely understand what you are going through," and the person's own mother was standing right next to him or her, it would have irritated me. That person couldn't possibly sympathize with me because he or she hadn't gone through it. The person could only empathize with my situation.

Here's what you should say to your client that denotes empathy, not sympathy: "I'm so sorry this happened to you. I can only imagine what you must be going through."

That's empathy.

Solve the problem.

Accept responsibility for what happened and solve the problem. Call whoever you need to call and get an answer for the client as fast as you can. Always give more than the client expects and don't make any promises that you can't keep.

Remember, their problem is very important to them. So even if you think their problem is unimportant, you must still respect them. Treat everyone you meet with the respect and dignity that they deserve. If you were standing there with that same problem, how would you want to be treated? What would you want the person to say to you?

Never burn bridges.

What do you do if someone e-mails you a scathing note? What if the person writes something that leaves you so angry you can't speak? Do you immediately e-mail the person and tell him or her what you think?

I was talking about this very subject at a conference recently with a colleague of mine named Jackie Farley, who is CEO and founder of Wise Women Incorporated. When I asked Jackie if that had ever happened to her, she told me the following story:

*I made the mistake of writing and hand-delivering a rather scathing note to a colleague one time after he had made a terribly sexist remark at a professional gathering. As soon as I walked away from him, I realized I had made a mistake. I grabbed my cell phone and called a long-time mentor, Laverne Wade, and asked her what I should do. She told me, "Never burn bridges. When you want to tell someone exactly what you think of them, always tear up the first, second, and third thing you write and then see if you feel the same way." I employ this advice regularly now—especially in this day of instantaneous e-mail and texting. Your anger is rarely well placed or well deserved at the moment it is at its peak, and it **never** places you in a positive light.*

My point exactly.

Be a GOOD Customer

Years ago I was traveling home from Las Vegas after teaching a concierge workshop. When I arrived at the airport, I was greeted with a delayed flight that caused me to miss my connection in Dallas. Sighing loudly, I went and stood in line to see if I could get another flight home.

As the line slowly crept forward, I started chatting with the people next to me and cracked a few jokes to lighten the mood a bit. My solution in situations like this has always been to laugh. No need to be angry about it, as it rarely does any good, so you might as well make the most of it.

When I finally got to the front of the line, I stood in stunned amazement as I listened to the guy in front of me yell at the young lady behind the desk. I've never seen anyone so angry! He was screaming so loud that the crowd behind me was silent as we all watched it play out in front of us. The young lady handled it well, and eventually, the guy stormed away.

Correct me if I'm wrong, but is it wise to yell at the person who has the power to send you home? We'll ignore the fact that it also wasn't her fault that the flight had been delayed. In my experience, shooting the messenger never works.

As luck would have it, I was next in line. When she motioned me to her station, I walked up and noticed that she was desperately trying not to cry and was attempting to pull herself together. So I smiled broadly at her, said good morning, and then placed my briefcase on the counter directly in front of her face so the people behind me couldn't see her. I then told her that it looked like she needed a break, so I encouraged her to take a few moments before she found me a flight. I could wait. My only thought was that if that were me, I would like a few minutes to get myself together.

You could see the gratitude in her eyes. She nodded her head in thanks, took a sip of water, sniffled a bit, and dabbed her eyes with a tissue. We then chatted about the man who was just there, and I got her to laugh a few times. After a few minutes went by, she started looking for a flight so I could go home. The next thing I knew, she handed me a first-class ticket! Since I was traveling coach, I was stunned by her gift. She smiled and told me how much those few minutes meant to her and then said she would like to buy me dinner as well. Then she handed me a gift certificate to a restaurant in the airport.

The moral here is this: To be a good customer, you should treat other people like you would like to be treated yourself. You just need to be nice to people.

The top seven things you should do to be a good customer

1.   Just be nice. Please treat the cashier or store clerk like a human being.

2.   Please don't snap your fingers or whistle to get someone's attention. It's extremely rude. Would you want someoneto do that to you.

3.   Treat people like you want to be treated.

4.   Don't talk on your cell phone when you are ordering food or standing at the checkout line. It's incredibly rude.

5.   Try to be patient if you are standing in line. Getting angry will not make the line move any faster.

6.   Remember your manners. Please and thank you go a long way in this world.

7.   Smile. It's contagious.

Don't Bring Your Baggage to Work

An Interview with Ron Giovanni, Cofounder of Triangle Concierge, Inc.

Ron has been working in the customer service, sales, and operations field for more than twenty-five years. He has been an entrepreneur for the last fourteen of those years.

Considering that you've been in customer service and sales for over twenty-five years now, if you were going to teach someone how to act like a concierge, what would you say to that person?

One of the first things is this: When you start your day, you can't start it out in the wrong frame of mind. You need to leave your "stuff" at home. If your job is to deal with dozens of people every day, then you're going to have to deal with many different personalities, whether you're a concierge, salesperson, or someone who works in a customer service call center. The key to dealing with all of these different personalities is to leave your baggage behind. You have to come in and perform at the highest level. If you're carrying that baggage, that anger from when something went wrong before you got to work, then that's going to come across to your customers. I know that you're going to meet many customers who are angry. The key is to keep a calm and even attitude with them. You have to be very nice and very kind because you want the customer to keep coming back.

No matter what happens, the customer has to be treated with respect and kindness. You have to listen to the customer. One of the biggest things that people forget to do when it comes to sales and customer service is that they forget to listen to what people are saying. Everyone wants to get their point across, and they tend to think that their idea and point is more important than yours. You have to understand that listening to your customers is the most important factor and is critical to your success.

So interrupting them is not an option, and being negative is not an option. You want people to adopt a positive attitude.

Absolutely! You're going to get more from your customers, and they're going to respect you more and want to do business with you more, if you come across as someone who cares about them and has empathy for them. They might be having a tough day, and you might be the only nice person that they have talked to all day! You might be the one that changes their whole attitude.

I think everyone who talks to the public should receive the proper training in customer service. From upper management all the way to the last employee, the entire company needs to be trained in customer service. In today's economy, you can't afford to lose customers, so good service is the key. Billions of dollars are spent each day on getting new customers, so what is going to get their attention? What is going to make them come back and do business with you again and again? Customer service. It's so cheap to offer excellent service.

It all starts with the top person in the company thinking about the customer. If the person at the top puts customer service first, then everyone else in the company will as well. It needs to go across the board.

This includes how to speak to the customer, correct?

Yes. You need to address your customers properly. Never call them by their first name, always reach out and offer them a warm greeting (shake their hand if they're standing in front of you), and always show them respect and attention. You can't tell them to "hold on" and "wait" and expect them to stand there. People today are looking for service immediately. You need to communicate with them. You can't expect them to wait on you. Also, if a customer is standing in front of you, then stop your conversation with your fellow employee and meet that customer's needs. There is a time and place for employees to talk to each other, but when a customer is on the phone or standing in front of you, then you need to focus on the customer and fulfill that customer's needs at the highest level. Even if you're talking to your boss! Service always comes first.

The concierge's job is to serve people. To find, to do, to get, to have, to know everything before a customer even gets there. It's important to get to know who your customers are because if you don't know that, then how are you going to know what their expectations are? If you don't know there expectations, then how are you going to deliver the services to them? You have to get to know them; you need to learn their name, what they like, and what they don't. It's important to know your customers because if you really know them, and you treat them nicely, then they'll be more inclined to do business with you again.

There are doormen all around the country who see people come in and out all day. They get to know every person in the building by name and what their needs are. A concierge does the same thing. Concierges do everything they can to understand their customers and their needs, and to know what will make their customer's day better.

There are such things as great customers, but there are also some incredibly rude and angry ones. What is your advice for people when they are faced with customers like these? How do you diffuse the situation?

The first thing I do is disarm them by being nice. It's hard for people to stay angry when you're being nice to them. When two people are fighting in front of you, do you stop it by behaving angry yourself? No, you diffuse the situation by being calm. Anger doesn't allow you to listen; in fact, it actually escalates the situation. You diffuse anger by being nice. You calmly talk them off the ledge, so to speak. Listen, even if they're yelling and screaming at you, as long as you have empathy for them and you're still nice to them, they'll calm down. You may not understand what they're going through, but you understand that they're having a problem or a bad day and they need something taken care of. You're there to do everything you can to appease them and fix their problem. They don't care how busy you are, nor do they care about your problems and the twenty thousand things that you have to do on your desk. They also don't care why your company didn't provide the service they wanted. People just want service. You apologize and then do what you need to do to fix it.

If something does happen, the first and most important thing is to be honest. You have to be honest, straightforward, and nice; talk in a calm voice and apologize. I've worked in many companies, and my job was to fix people's problems. Whenever someone had a problem, he or she gave it to me and I always fixed the problem by finding a solution that satisfied the person. Notice what I just said—you need to satisfy the customer, not you. It's all about satisfying the customer. It's not about finding a solution that works for both of you; it's about finding a solution that works for the customer.

I remember times when I couldn't fix the situation, but because I had developed a relationship with my customers, they trusted me to find a solution that would work. They knew that I would do the best that I could for them. Again, it has to do with building relationships and being nice to people. However, don't drop the ball. If you say that you're going to do something, then get it done no matter what.

Do you have any last pieces of advice for my readers?

My biggest piece of advice is this: Make sure that when you start your day, you start on an even balance with a great attitude. Don't bring your baggage to work because you can hear it on the phone. People can actually hear you smile, and they can hear you frown. Don't sigh because they'll hear that, too.

Ultimately, you have to be honest, straightforward, kind, and respectful. You should never raise your voice, and you should never speak down to people. If you're nice to them, I guarantee you that they'll remember it because we all remember how people make us feel.

Chapter 11

International Protocol

Key to Excellence:

Know how to communicate with people from other cultures

A number of years ago, I was flying home and arrived at the airport (my last airport story, I promise). It had been a long day, and I was ready to go home. I got into line at the terminal to get my ticket, and as I stood there, I found myself surrounded by a group of Japanese businessmen. Now when I say surrounded, I mean surrounded. We were standing shoulder to shoulder with their arms and shoulders actually touching mine. Since I'm a typical American and like to have some personal space around me, this situation made me uncomfortable. So I simply stepped out of line and moved to the back.

A little while later, I was sitting comfortably in an aisle seat on the airplane. When I got settled, I politely nodded to the businessman next to me. Since it was obvious that he didn't speak English, I opened the book that I had brought with me and started to read. About thirty minutes later, he decided to visit the restroom. So he stood up, lifted his leg, and tried to crawl over my body. Since I generally don't like people I don't know crawling over my lap, I immediately stood and held my hand out indicating he should wait. I then politely motioned him to go by. I sat down more than a little irritated and tried to go back to my book.

I was ready when he arrived a few minutes later, but before I had time to stand up, the leg came up a second time and he tried to crawl over me again. So I repeated the performance I gave a few minutes before and stood, held out my hand, and motioned him to go back to his seat.

After it was all over, I quietly sat there and tried to breathe. I attempted to calm myself by reading my book, but after I read the same sentence four times, I knew that it was impossible. So I put my book down and glanced around the cabin. Imagine my surprise when I saw all the Japanese doing the exact same thing as my seat mate. My anger dissolved in a heartbeat. I immediately realized that a gesture they consider to be polite and normal in Japan, we consider rude here in the United States. How can you be mad at that?

So my journey into the world of international protocol began. I purchased a few books, visited Web sites, and made absolutely sure that I checked out the customs of my clients' countries before I met with them. I'm not saying I always get it right, but I'm trying.

This leads me to international gestures. Please be careful here because a gesture that is common in the United States might be terribly rude in another country. For example, if someone asks you for directions in the United States, you might raise your right hand and point with your finger. However, pointing is considered extremely rude in many countries. If you have to point, then point using an open hand with your thumb curled into the palm of your hand and your other four fingers locked together.

Here are some examples that I pulled from the wonderful book *Kiss, Bow or Shake Hands* by Terri Morrison and Wayne A. Conway. The book lists dozens of countries and protocols:

Talking with your hands

In the United Kingdom, it is considered impolite to talk with your hands in your pockets. Also, Brits keep their hands on the table when eating (as opposed to Americans who put their hands in their laps).

Touching

In Finland, China, and the United Kingdom, people don't like to touch each other in public, so touching them on the arm (or any other place) will make them VERY uncomfortable.

Gestures

In Japan, even the slightest gesture can mean something, so make sure you don't make any expansive hand or arm gestures. Although pushing your way through a crowd is extremely impolite here in the U.S., it's not in Japan. In fact, I'm told that it's the only way you can get on the Japanese subways.

Eye contact

In the U.S., direct eye contact is a sign of honesty. However, in Latin America, prolonged eye contact is considered aggressive, so if clients are not looking directly at you when they are speaking, then they are being polite. In Japan, prolonged eye contact is considered rude, as is pointing.

Respect their comfort zone

Americans have a few odd quirks, and this is one of them. When we stand next to someone, we like to have a two- to three-foot comfort zone around our body at all times. If someone invades that personal space, we'll even go so far as to take a step back to reestablish our personal comfort zone.

Not everyone feels this way though. Latin Americans like to stand close when they're speaking to you, which is hard for an American because we'll instinctively want to step back to keep our distance from them, which the Latin American will find rude. Greeks are expressive and will stand close to you and might even kiss you when you first meet them.

What other quirks do Americans have? We'll talk about anything—our family, our kids, our career, even sex, just don't ask us how much money we make. Americans hate to tell people how much money they earn. Many Europeans don't care and will tell you their earnings in a heartbeat. Americans? Not so much.

Heads and hands

When someone from Germany shakes your hand, it's often accompanied by a nod of the head. Germans find it insulting if you speak to them with your hands in your pockets.

Chewing gum

In France, Poland, and New Zealand, it's considered extremely rude to chew gum in public.

Winking

Please don't wink. It has a different meaning to people living outside of the U.S., and it might be misinterpreted.

Left hands

In the Muslim and Hindu world, your left hand is considered unclean. So use your right hand as much as possible.

Feet

Feet are considered unclean in South Africa and India, so don't touch anything with your feet. If you do, apologize immediately. In Singapore, you shouldn't sit with your legs crossed because it shows the bottom of your feet, which is considered extremely rude.

Gifts

Be careful when you are giving gifts, especially when it comes to color. For example, the color for mourning is black in the United States, red in parts of Africa, and white in Asia. Never give anything made from cowhide to Hindus, as cows are considered sacred.

I could go on and on, but I won't, of course. This was just a small sample to give you a little taste of international protocol and how important it is. If you want to be a truly great concierge, then you must have a good working knowledge of other people's customs around the world.

One last thought. If you don't understand the person because of his heavy accent, please don't pretend that you do. Honesty is always the best policy. Smile and apologize, and then gently tell the person you're having a hard time understanding him. Ask him to slow down a bit. The key here is to make the person realize that you are genuinely trying to understand and help him.

For more information about international protocol, I suggest that you purchase Kiss, Bow or Shake Hands by Morrison and Conway. You can also visit their Web site at www.kissboworshakehands.com. I actually have a copy of the book on my desk and will read the necessary chapter when I have an international client flying in so I know what to say and do. Another great protocol site that I use quite often is www.kwintessential.co.uk.

It's the three C's:
Confidence, Courtesy and Common Sense

An Interview with Dallas Teague Snider, CMP

*Ms. Snider has been in the hospitality management and meeting plan-
ning field for more than twenty years, and is currently a Certified Business Etiquette and International Protocol Consultant. She is the owner
of Make Your Best Impression: A division of Leadreferrals Sales & Mar-
keting Services, Inc.*

*If you were going to teach a concierge, what would you tell him or her
about international protocol?*

The most important thing people need to understand is that concierges anticipate the needs of their guests and exceed their expectations. This is their ultimate goal. When it comes to international
guests, you have to understand their culture and customs. You really need to do some research on your guests and their customs so
that you can learn what is and is not appropriate in their country.
You need to know what they consider to be respectful, disrespect-
ful, and what a proper greeting should be. Also, with international
guests you should always lean toward an air of formality and being
respectful. You never want to be casual, or address them by their
first name unless they request that you do so.

*What if you don't do your homework and an international guest just
appears in front of you?*

This is what I think is so fascinating. Fifty-five percent of the message that we transmit to someone is based on our appearance and
our body language; 38 percent comes from our vocal tones, pacing,

and inflections; and only 7 percent of the verbal message comes from words used. You can say so much with a smile, having an open appearance to convey the message that you are trying to get them to understand. When guests appear unexpectedly, it can be easy to feel unprepared. If you show that you are trying, they are certainly going to be more receptive to your mishaps rather than thinking that you don't care about them.

Also, please don't make unnecessary gestures like talking with your hands that might be misconstrued as rude. A gesture that is polite in the United States might mean something totally different in their country, so be careful. It comes down to having confidence in yourself. If you are a concierge, and you know that you are going to have frequent international guests, then it's your responsibility to know how to treat each guest and make that guest feel comfortable. Do your research. Know what types of gifts are acceptable and what are not. Know how people from their country prefer to be greeted. There are a lot of books and Web sites that you can access to learn about other cultures so that you can have a general idea of what to do.

Let me give you an example, if you know you have a lot of customers who speak Spanish, it would be reasonable to do some research to find out what type of greeting they prefer, provide staff members with some general phrases they might use (such as saying please and thank you in Spanish) as well as having several staff on duty who speak fluent Spanish.

If you can learn the greetings and the things that show respect to them, and be kind and friendly, then your international guests will realize that you are a kind person and it will break down the barriers. One of the things that is so difficult for Americans in the international area is that many people think we are arrogant and that we don't respect their cultures. If you try and speak their language, especially in France, then they'll be kind to you and they'll really appreciate it. So it's those little things that will make the difference. They all realize that America is a land unto its own, whereas if you are in Europe, you have to learn many languages because it's like going from state to state. Europeans all learn about different cultures, and many speak more than one language.

We need to step out of our comfort zone, and we need to respect other cultures. When we visit their country, we shouldn't expect them to adhere to our culture and customs.

The goal here is to be courteous and kind. It's the three C's:

1. **Confidence** — knowing how to act in a given situation.

2. **Courtesy** — being kind to people. Consideration, cooperation, and generosity.

3. **Common Sense** — common sense is one of those things that people tend to forget. Trust your intuition. If it doesn't feel right, then don't do it.

As far as the international arena goes, I think it's crucial to understand that it's your job to know how to talk and do business with people from other cultures. You should do the research and know the Web sites where you can find out this information.

When there is a challenge or an obstacle, you should exceed their expectations because often clients will forgive the mishap and forget what happened (instead of telling ten people what a bad experience they had). Go above and beyond. Why do you go to a restaurant where the atmosphere is not wonderful, the food is pretty good, but the service is great? Because the service is great. They'll remember how you made them feel, and they'll remember that feeling when they see you again.

Customer service is not optional. When you believe that, the results will come tenfold.

To read more about Ms. Snider, you can visit her Web site at www.makeyourbestimpression.com.

**You cannot improve one thing by 1000%,
but you can improve 1000 little things by 1%.**

— Jan Carlzon

Chapter 12

Internal Customer Service

Key to Excellence:

Be nice to your fellow staff members and employees. Happy employees treat their customers better.

While most of this book is focused on external customer service and how you treat your customers, it will do you no good if you don't practice internal customer service that goes above and beyond.

Companies around the world invest a lot of time and money on external customer service so that they can get more customers. Unfortunately, most forget to pay attention to internal customer service—which is how their employees are treating each other. If you really want to act like a true concierge and offer service that goes above and beyond, then you must do it both internally and externally.

The Anti-Customer Service Department

I had to return something to a large retail store a while back. After walking around the store for a while, I soon found the customer service sign. Underneath it was a woman talking on her cell phone.

I walked up and stood in front of her. I didn't say anything because I didn't want to interrupt her phone call. I assumed she was on a personal call because she was using her cell phone, so I waited patiently for her to finish the call. We'll just ignore the fact that you shouldn't be making personal calls on your cell phone while sitting at a customer service desk.

So I stood there.

And stood there.

Finally, after a few minutes went by, I politely said, "Excuse me . . ."

She then said into the phone, and no I'm not making this up, "Hold on a minute; I have to get rid of a customer standing in front of me."

Excuse me?

I immediately asked for her supervisor. The girl made a sour face and told me to "hold on a second."

When her manager finally came to the desk, I returned my item and then told her what happened and suggested that her staff receive some customer service training. Now, if this young lady was not trained properly because her supervisor lacked the appropriate training in customer service, then it's just bad service from top to bottom. Internal and external customer service spreads across the entire company and reaches everyone. It starts at the top and trickles all the way down to the very last employee.

If you feel that your personal calls are more important than the customers who are standing right in front of you, then may I suggest that you not sit directly underneath a sign that says "customer service." Staff should be focused on the customers and readily available to customers. Some solid customer service training could go a long way in solving the problem here.

Here's the real problem: How do you get this woman to really care about her job? How can you turn her around and get her to provide incredible, over-the-top customer service?

If I had her in one of my training sessions, I would look her directly in the eye and tell her that you never know who might be standing in front of you. It could be your next boss. In fact, you might impress this person so much that she hires you on the spot. What if you're working at a fast food restaurant? The great service you give to that regular customer might be the key that lands you a new job at that same customer's company. Don't burn your bridges because you never know who you are talking to.

Great words, but it still might not be enough to get her to care. Further, since everyone does not have the same definition of great customer service, it makes it even harder.

One way to get her to care is to offer good internal customer service. In other words, you should treat your fellow staff member's right! A truly great concierge treats everyone the same way—from customers to fellow staff members, a concierge is nice to everyone and treats them all with respect. A great concierge is warm, friendly, and approachable to everyone.

According to a survey conducted by David J. Lux, Steve M. Jex, and Curtiss P. Hansen on "Factors Influencing Employee Perceptions of Customer Service Climate," published in the *Journal of Market-Focused Management*, it was found "that rewarding employees for service excellence, allowing their voice to be heard by upper management, providing employees with the information and technology needed to do their jobs, providing adequate training to customer contact employees, allowing employees enough time to get their tasks done, and providing a work environment conducive to getting work done are all positively associated with employee perceptions of customer service climate."

Many companies around the United States respect the secret of "just be nice" and have put it into practice every day. Companies such as Google, The Four Seasons Hotels and Resorts, The Ritz Carlton, Ben and Jerry's, SAS, and Chick-fil-A all provide over-the-top customer service both internally and externally. Internally, they keep their employees happy with some great work/life benefits such as concierge services, job sharing, on-site daycare, on-site personal chefs, and the like.

S. Truett Cathy, founder of Chick-fil-A, practices these principles. "Exemplary service begins with hiring the right people. The closer top management is to the customer, the more successful an organization is likely to be," says Cathy, who treats his employees with great respect and offers college scholarships to employees.

By helping employees better themselves, Cathy is creating employee loyalty, which causes them to be more satisfied with their jobs, which in turn leads to a high employee retention rate. Cathy's employees treat the customers better because they're happier with their jobs, which ultimately leads to bigger profits for the company. "We've been able to excel by just being kind. Courtesy is very cheap, and it pays great dividends," says Cathy.

In an article called "Creating a Motivated Workforce," Donald McNerney wrote, "A good work environment, a safe place to work, a feeling of security, opportunities to progress in the company, and how management treats employees would be weighed by the average person much more than money."

Treating your staff, fellow employees, and customers nicely and giving them the respect they deserve will raise your bottom line.

So how well are you working with the other people in your company? Does your department work well with other departments? Are your people happy? As stated above, happy employees treat their customers better and make great team players.

A few tips to help you offer better internal customer service:

Provide clear guidelines.

Everyone should know what is expected of them. Guidelines should be clear and concise.

Always go above and beyond.

Don't just "do" the task; take it a step further whenever you can. Put yourself in the other person's shoes and ask yourself how you would want it done.

Be polite and mind your manners.

Always say "please" and "thank you," and never lose your temper!

Answer internal calls and e-mails.

Answer your calls and e-mails as quickly as you would external calls from your customers.

Never complain about the company or a fellow employee in front of a customer.

For example, if you are a receptionist, please be aware that the entire waiting room can hear your conversation.

Keep the lines of communication open.

It's difficult to solve problems when you don't know what they are. Have social events so that you can get to know each other and talk. Be nice to each other.

Follow up meetings.

After a project is finished, have a meeting to consider what happened. Discuss everything from the good to the bad to the ugly. This is also a good time to find out if anyone is harboring resentment about the project. I've found that resentments can be extremely destructive if you don't talk about them.

Put yourself in their shoes.

Put yourself in their shoes and try to imagine what doing their job must be like. Walking a mile in someone else's shoes will change your perspective and will most likely cause you to rethink the situation. In fact, take this idea further and do it for your customers as well. Be a customer and go through all the channels to see what it's like on the other end. I think the answers you get will surprise you.

This, of course, leads me right back to the great secret of the concierge industry that I wrote about in the first chapter of this book:

Just be nice to each other.

They'll Always Remember How You Made Them Feel

An Interview with Doug Cook
Concierge Worldwide, Birmingham, Alabama

Mr. Cook has been in the hospitality industry for more than thirty years and is the owner of Concierge Worldwide in Birmingham, Alabama.

If you were going to teach concierges, what would you tell them?

I've been in the hospitality industry since 1979, and I think it boils down to a basic premise. If you don't inherently enjoy serving other people and taking care of their needs, my feeling has always been that you are in the wrong industry. You have to like what you do. You have to be approachable. You have to be aware and anticipate their needs. You have to be able to read situations and people so that you can see whether or not they need help with something because often they don't know who to ask about it.

Remember, even if you do the absolute best that you can, sometimes it won't be enough. Just know that you can't please everyone 100 percent of the time. Sometimes they might just be having a bad day and nothing you do will make them happy. All you can do is your very best.

I work as a concierge in a hospital, and the best part is being there for people to talk to. Sometimes I'm the only happy face they see all day, and often they just want to talk. It's rewarding. They might not remember what I said to them, but they'll always remember how they felt when they were talking to me at my desk.

I think the key is that you need to instill the attitude of personal service into every employee and make sure everyone pays close attention to the customers. You need to be proactive. Take ownership of the client's problem, and once you do, you'll see it through to the end.

To read more about Mr. Cook, you can visit his Web site at www.concierge-worldwide.net.

Chapter 13

How to Present a Positive Attitude

Key to Excellence:

You need to be positive.

If you want to act like a truly great concierge who provides over-the-top, five-star customer service, then you must do three things:

1. You need to be nice to people. You should be warm, friendly, and approachable.

2. You need to be positive! Lose all the gloom and doom thoughts because clients need you to be positive and focused on the task at hand, especially if they are the ones being negative.

3. You need to be able to leave your "personal stuff" at home. Clients don't need to hear about your life because they want to talk to you about theirs.

That's it. Simple, right?

Unfortunately, being positive all the time is much easier said than done. You have to stay positive and be able to solve all the client's troubles in an instant. Plus you have to do it with a smile on your face, even if your own world is toppling down around you. No matter what the situation is at home, you need to be positive. There are no exceptions here.

I practice what I preach. I teach a great many workshops each year, and every once in a while, I have to teach one sick. You get through it with a smile on your face, hot tea, and the occasional Tylenol. Then there was the time I had to teach a two-day workshop knowing that when I got home we had to put our dog to sleep. Staying focused and positive with that on my mind was one of the hardest things I've ever done. The attendees never knew what was going on because I took a deep breath, centered myself, stuffed my grief into the back corner of my mind, put a huge smile on my face, and taught the class. The show must go on no matter what.

Why do you do this? Because how someone makes you FEEL will stay with you forever. You might not remember what a concierge did for you, but you will remember how they treated you and how they made you feel.

That's the key to excellence.

In fact, that last paragraph is so important, I'm going to repeat it:

You might not remember what a concierge did for you, but you will remember how they treated you and how they made you feel.

How to Put the Negative Behind You

According to Brian Tracy, "Optimism is the one quality more associated with success and happiness than any other." Put simply, if you dwell on the negative and look at your life as being "half empty," then the negativity will bury you.

There is a spiritual principle called the Law of Focus that says what you put your attention to grows. If you dwell on the positive, positive will come back to you and will grow exponentially. However, if you dwell on the negative and see it all around you, then it will slam into your life like a runaway train. So if you are the type of person who tends to think negatively all the time, then I strongly suggest that you learn how to duck because negative stuff will start slamming into you fast, if it hasn't already.

If you want to be a truly GREAT concierge, then you have to stop being negative all the time.

When my two sons were small, I used to take them to our neighborhood pool. I remember one time in particular when the pool had just opened for the season. When we got there, I quickly found some chairs near some acquaintances of ours and started to chat with them as the boys swam.

About twenty minutes went by when I began to notice that everything my friend talked about had a negative slant to it. First, it was complaining about a particular teacher at school, then it was about the lack of time in life in general, and on and on it went. She said nothing positive—all negative, complaining about this and that. When she got to politics, I decided that it was enough and quickly excused myself and jumped into the pool.

As I swam around the pool, I couldn't help but hear other conversations. Imagine my surprise when I found that they too were mostly negative! Curious now, I walked over to the soda machine and said, "How are you?" to some other neighbors. Their reply? "Tired. You know how it goes." Not exactly negative, but certainly not positive either.

So now I was REALLY curious! Was it just that it was the end of the week and everyone was tired and grumpy? I decided to test it, so for the next few days I really paid attention to everything I saw and heard to see how much negativity there really was.

Let me tell you I didn't have to try very hard.

First, I went to the grocery store. As I waited for the cashier to tally my groceries, I started chatting with her, and soon I was being told a story about her trip to Japan. Since she's a blonde, she complained that her trip was horrible because some Japanese wanted to touch her hair.

That evening I switched on the evening news and was presented with thirty minutes of murder, robberies, and child abductions. In between these heartwarming stores, I listened to commercials about weight loss, adult ADD, and a new drug that the advertiser said everyone should take (but had some small side effects like nausea and sometimes death).

After the news, I flipped around and found some television shows including *Law and Order and CSI*, whose story lines are generated from news headlines. All great shows but hardly positive. It seems I was surrounded by murder, rape, and the dregs of society—all in primetime. I settled for a *Touched by an Angel* rerun and went to bed.

When I woke up the next morning, I continued to pay attention. The first thing on my agenda that morning was a visit to the post office. When I arrived, I was greeted at the door by an identity theft poster. I then went to a department store to pick up a new bathing suit for one of my sons and noticed that the store had TV monitors all over the place. As I looked at a monitor, I saw a story about how to prevent your child from being abducted.

Are you seeing a pattern here? I'm not making this up; it really happened.

Okay, let's try the computer. Maybe that's better.

After logging on, I took a look at my home page at MSN and I saw a story about Al-Qaida, a report about a woman found strangled, and a weather-related story about a nasty tornado.

And don't forget my e-mail. I had my usual number of SPAM e-mails, which generally includes sales pitches and various offers about Viagra. Let's not forget the e-mail from a gentleman in Nigeria who wants to wash $1 million through my checking account and wants me to send him the number. Of course, he'll give me half.

Uh-huh. I totally believe you.

Later that day, I went to get my mail and saw my neighbor outside doing some yard work. When I stopped to say hello, he asked how I was doing. I replied, "I'm doing really great today; thank you for asking!" I don't think he was expecting me to say that because he stopped what he was doing and looked at me like I had just escaped from an insane asylum. I laughed, told him I would see him later, and went into my house.

When did it become politically incorrect to tell people something positive?

By the end of the second day, I was feeling physically sick and incredibly tired. I went to bed early and asked my husband Ron to put the boys to bed. I just wanted to lie down, pull the covers over my head, and forget about it all.

So what did I learn from this little test? I learned that thinking negatively can mess up your mind.

I felt like I had been dragged into a negative world filled with greed, fear, and hatred. A world where you always lack money and never achieve your life's dreams because you are too fat, too thin, too sick, going to be sick, need a job, or lost a job.

I felt that my brain had been so saturated with negativity that I was in danger of becoming physically sick! By the end of the second day, I was yelling at my kids, bickering with my husband, and grumpy to everyone.

So I drank a cup of hot tea, took a bath, and went to bed. The test was officially over. Two days was more than enough for me.

On the third day, I decided to visit the same places I had gone to during my little test to see what positives I could find there. First, I went to the pool and sat down in a chair. As I watched, I saw people laughing and smiling, and children playing in the pool with huge smiles on their faces. The sound of happy children playing is really one of life's greatest sounds and put an immediate smile on my face.

I then went to the grocery store to pick up some milk and saw aisle after aisle filled with food, supplies, drinks, and fresh produce. I saw people chatting and smiling, and two children happily eating a messy chocolate doughnut.

I went back to the post office and started to chat with the woman in front of me who was mailing a large package to her son in the military. She was sending his unit some things she thought they might need.

I logged onto the Internet and received a wonderful e-mail from a friend called "The Positive Side of Life." I then received an e-mail from an old friend of mine whom I've known for more than forty years. It always puts a smile on my face when I hear from her.

As I was leaving the house to pick up my boys from school, I saw my neighbor again and I asked him how he was doing. He turned and looked at me with a big smile on his face and replied, "I'm doing really great today; thank you for asking!"

That evening, I turned on the evening news, and watched an extremely beautiful story about a woman moving into her first home—built by the wonderful organization Habitat for Humanity. Then the weather came on, and I was told that bright sunshine would be in our area for the next few days. Later that evening, I watched a rerun of that great show on ABC called *Extreme Makeover Home Edition*. In seven days, they completely changed a needy family's home and life.

Remember the Law of Focus that states what you put your attention to grows? Certainly the case here.

I put my attention to all the negative "stuff" that I was assaulted with for a few days, and it slammed into me so hard that I wanted to cry from it all. It got so bad that I saw it everywhere I went. It could make a person seriously paranoid. However, when I placed my attention on the positive, it grew, too. It was like it had suddenly stopped raining, and the warm sun came out.

So how do you remain positive in a negative world?

Here are a few tips:

Surround yourself with positive people.

Treat others like you want to be treated—positively—with positive encouragement and thoughts.

Turn off the news as much as possible.

Turn off the news and try and avoid newspapers, although you should scan the headlines so that you know what's going on in the world.

Write it down!

Write down all the positive things that have happened to you in the last month and post them where you can see them. See your life as a success by looking at all the positive things that you've done.

Display positive posters and art.

Put a positive/inspirational poster over your desk. You can also put a "plus" sign or the words "stay positive" over your desk to remind you to be positive.

Read some inspirational books.

Help people out.

Turn someone else's negative day into a positive—help them out!

Now please know that I'm not telling you to blindly ignore the reality of the world. I'm telling you that you can see that reality and also see the POSITIVES as well. The world can indeed be a cruel place. Crime, poverty, and illness seem to be everywhere, but the world also can be a beautiful place filled with love, warmth, compassion, and prosperity.

Do you see the glass as half-full or half-empty?

Negative things will happen in the world. They happen to all of us. But look at it this way: positive things will happen as well. Good things will happen to you. Joy will find you! It goes back to the laws of physics:

1. For every action there is an equal and opposite reaction.

2. Energy attracts like energy.

If we put out negative thoughts and actions and constantly focus on the negative, we will ATTRACT negative back to us. It will be all that we see. Conversely, if we put out positive thoughts and try our best to see the positive, then we will attract the positive back. We think it, we say it, and then we do it. It's as simple as that. Our thoughts create our reality.

We live in a world that seems to focus on the negative. So be it. I, however, refuse to be negative and will continue to try and remain positive as much as possible. I've had my share of bad times, trust me; I wrote the book on that one. The good news is that I don't have to stay that way if I don't choose to. I choose to look at the glass as half full, one day at a time.

I choose to go above and beyond.

**Unless you have 100% customer satisfaction...
you must improve.**

— Horst Schulz,
former Ritz Carlton chief executive officer

Chapter 14

Doing the Right Thing

Key to Excellence:

**Customer service is not what you do;
it's who you are. It's a way of life.**

Now that you're all pumped up and positive, I have one more thing to talk to you about while I have your attention. We need to talk about how you should behave when you're "off" duty.

For me, customer service is a way of life. It's not what you do; it's who you are. It's something that comes from deep inside of you. I can always pick out the people who practice this philosophy because they're the ones who hold doors open for people, say crazy things like "please" and "thank you," and pick up their garbage when they leave the movie theater. Plain and simple, they're just nice people. They're warm, friendly, approachable, easy to talk to, and are quite adept at turning lemons into lemonade.

It's a philosophy that we should all live by.

A few summers ago I was walking off a soccer field after a game when I noticed a pile of empty water bottles on the side of the road. There were at least thirty of them, all piled on top of each other. Since no one was picking them up, and every parent was just walking by them, I decided to take a few minutes and dispose of them. So I bent over and picked up as many as I could. Soon my husband pitched in to help. As we worked to pick them all up, we wondered which team could have left them.

As I reached for the last three bottles, an elderly gentleman stopped and looked at us. It was obvious that he had listened to our conversation because he immediately defended himself by saying, "Those bottles don't belong to our team."

Although my arms were completely full of bottles, I took the time to stop and answer him. I smiled and politely replied by saying I was sure that they didn't.

He then asked why I was picking them up since they clearly didn't belong to my team either.

I looked him directly in the eye and said, "Because it's the right thing to do."

He just looked at me like I was a crazy person, muttered "good for you," and walked to his car never once offering to help. Who did he think was going to pick them up? The guy who mows the lawn?

You just can't make this stuff up.

Doing the right thing, even if it's a small thing, is never wrong. In fact, even when you are absolutely certain that no one will ever find out about what you've done, you should do it anyway.

It's the Little Things That Count

You know, in life quite often it's the little things that count. Everyone knows that doing little things for your spouse or loved one always makes a huge impact. Bringing home flowers for no reason at all, surprising someone at work with a cake, or offering a simple smile goes a long way with people.

I'll never forget the time I held a door open for an elderly couple coming out of a restaurant. They smiled at me politely and shuffled out. However, before I could walk into the restaurant, I found myself holding the door for two twenty-year-olds who just pushed by me like they owned the world. Four more people followed after that. You would think that one of them would have thought to say thank you. None did. I was stunned.

This leads me to entitlement. When did it become popular to believe that you are entitled to everything life has to offer, but you feel no compulsion to help anyone out? It's like people are living life on a one-way street and have adopted the attitude "it's all about me" as an acceptable way of life.

I think it goes without saying that if you're nice to people, generally they'll be nice back. You get back what you put out into the world. If you keep running across people who treat people badly, and you run across them all the time, then I humbly suggest that you look inside of yourself because your mind creates your reality.

So do the right thing people. Help someone out, hold open a door, smile, carry someone's bag, let someone go in front of you in the grocery line—just do the right thing.

Diplomacy

While you are doing the right thing, remember to use diplomacy and tact when you're speaking to people so you don't offend them.

I used to work with someone years ago who prided herself on being straightforward and honest with people. The unfortunate thing was that she tended to come off sounding like a bully and often spoke her mind without considering the other person's feelings.

I agree that you should be honest with people, absolutely right. However, I think you should do it with a large dose of diplomacy and tact.

In today's world, it's incredibly important to offer your clients customer service that goes above and beyond. Would you want to continue to go to a restaurant if the staff treated you badly every time you went there? Would you want to work with a company who had a receptionist that snapped at you? I doubt it.

Today, more than ever, we need to learn how to offer great customer service because that's the way to turn people into regular customers. If you're nice to me and go out of your way to help me, then not only will I come back, but I'm going to tell three of my best friends to use your services.

The real key to being an incredible concierge is to go above and beyond everyone else and become extraordinary.

Chapter 15

My Top 20 Keys to Excellence in Customer Service

My Top 20 Keys to Excellence in Customer Service

(The First Six Are the Most Important)

1. Just be nice!

2. Just be nice!

3. Just be nice!

4. Just be nice!

5. Just be nice!

6. Just be nice!

7. Exceed their expectations.

8. You need to go five steps beyond, not just one.

9. Become an expert at speaking to people.

10. Always mind your manners—no exceptions.

11. Always dress for success.

12. Think and always be ready for anything.

13. Be warm, friendly and approachable.

14. Communicating well is critical.

15. Treat people as you would like to be treated.

16. Know how to communicate with people from other cultures.

17. Be nice to your fellow staff members and employees because happy employees treat their customers better.

18. You need to be positive!

19. Customer service is not what you do; it's who you are. It's a way of life.

20. Oh and one more thing—just be nice.

Bibliography

Books

Horrell, Ed. *The Kindness Revolution*. American Management Association, 2006.

Morrison, Terri, and Wayne A. Conaway. *Kiss, Bow, or Shake Hands*. Avon, MA: Adams Media, 1995, 2006.

Articles

Andrew, Kevin. "The Handshake." *Nonverbal Communication Web Project*. http://soc302.tripod.com/soc_302rocks/id8.html.

"April 25, 1945: East Meets West." www.lindsayfincher. com/2004/04/april_25_1945_east_meets_west.html.

Borenstein, Seth. "Harvard Study: Nice Guys Actually Finish First." Associated Press. www.USAToday.com (March 2008).

Cardillo, Donna, RN, MA. "The Uncommon Handshake." Nursing Spectrum Nurse Wire (www.nurse.com). Copyright 2005. All rights reserved. Used with permission.

Chaplin, William F., PhD, Jeffrey B. Phillips, Jonathan D. Brown, Nancy R. Clanton, and Jennifer L. Stein. "Handshaking, Gender, Personality and First Impressions." *Journal of Personality and Social Psychology*, 79, no. 1. University of Alabama.

Ey, Craig. "Chick-fil-A Chairman Says Business, Morals Can Co-Exist." *Birmingham Business Journal* (March 3, 2008).

Field, Audrey. "Present a Professional Image: A Professional Image Is Especially Important for Home-Based Businesses." http://sbinfocanada.about.com/od/marketing/qt/profimageaf.htms.

Fenson, Sarah. "Align Your Actions with Your Words." Inc.com (September 2000). www.inc.com/articles/2000/09/20279.html.

Gardner, Donald G., Linn Van Dyne, and Jon L. Pierce. "The Effects of Pay Level on Organization-Based Self-Esteem and Performance: A Field Study (Analysis of Employees' Performance)." *Journal of Occupational and Organizational Psychology* (September 2004).

Goldman, Lynda. "Body Language: Seven Secrets for Connecting with Nonverbal Communication." http://ezinearticles.com/?Body-Language---7-Secrets-for-Connecting-with-Non-Verbal-Communication&id=800821.

Harrison, Craig. "Turning Customer Service Inside Out! How Poor Internal Customer Service Affects External Customers." www.principledprofit.com/index.html.

Hayward, Mark. "The Importance of Nonverbal Communication: Ten Things Your Handshake Says About You." www.mytropicalescape.com. (November 2007).

"International Business Etiquette." www.kwintessential.co.uk/articles/international-business-etiquette.html.

Kissell, Joe, and Morgen Jahnke. "The Handshake, Coming to Grips with Gestures of Greeting." *Interesting Thing of the Day* (September 2004).

Lux, David J., Steve M. Jex, and Curtiss P. Hansen. "Factors Influencing Employee Perceptions of Customer Service Climate." *Journal of Market-Focused Management* 1, no. 1 (March 1996).

Maier, R. "Customer Wait Time." www.ezinearticles.com (December 2006).

McGregor, Jena, with Frederick F. Jespersen and Megan Tucker in New York and Dean Foust. "Customer Service Champs." *Business Week* (March 2007).

McNerney, Donald J. "Creating a Motivated Workforce." *HR Focus* (August 1996).

Mehrabian's communication study. http://changingminds.org/explanations/behaviors/body_language/mehrabian.htm.

Partenheimer, David. "Your Handshake May Provide More Information to Others Than You Think." *APA News Release* (July 2000).

Pemberton-Sikes, Diana. "Professional Attire: Is What You're Wearing Hurting Your Career?" *The Sideroad: Practical Advice Straight from the Experts.*

"Remembering Their Name." http://changingminds.org/techniques/conversation/name/remembering_name.htm.

Robertson, Kelley. "The Power of a Name." www.businessknowhow.com/growth/remember-name.htm.

Scanlin, Amy. "Customer Service 101." *Fitness Management Magazine* (October 2004).

Smith, Gregory P. "Customer Service Success: Front-line Employees Are Key to Success." www.about.com. http://humanresources.about.com/od/customerservice/a/serve_customers.htm.

"The Customer Service Elite." http://bwnt.businessweek.com/interactive_reports/customer_satisfaction/index.asp.

"Using Body Language." http://changingminds.org.

Web Sites

http://changingminds.org

http://en.wikipedia.org/wiki/Handshake

www.bodylanguagetraining.com/